LifeLight

"In Him was life, and the life was the light of men." John 1:4

Haggai/Zechariah/Malachi

LEADERS GUIDE

CONCORDIA PUBLISHING HOUSE • SAINT LOUIS

"The prophet's greatness was his ability to lead God's people who were initially too busy with their own concerns to concentrate on rebuilding the temple. Zechariah enabled the faithful remnant to pick up the pieces of the exile and embrace God's promises that would come to fruition in Christ Jesus."

—*From "Who's Who in the Book of Zechariah" in the enrichment magazine.*

This painting of the Prophet Zechariah is by Michelangelo Buonarroti. Found on the ceiling of the Sistine Chapel, it is believed to be a portrait of Pope Julius II.

Copyright © 2013 Concordia Publishing House
3558 S. Jefferson Ave., St. Louis, MO 63118-3968
1-800-325-3040 • www.cph.org

All rights reserved. No part of this publication may be reproduced, stored in a retrieval system, or transmitted, in any form or by any means, electronic, mechanical, photocopying, recording, or otherwise, without the prior written permission of Concordia Publishing House.

Written by Mark B. Stirdivant

Edited by Brian Chisamore

Field testing coordinated by Denise Muhly and Our Savior Lutheran Church, Cheyenne, WY

Cover art: The Prophet Zechariah, Sistine Chapel. Erich Lessing/Art Resource, NY

Unless otherwise indicated, Scripture quotations from the ESV Bible® (The Holy Bible, English Standard Version®), copyright © 2001 by Crossway Bibles, a publishing ministry of Good News Publishers. Used by permission. All rights reserved.

Quotations marked KJV are from the King James or Authorized Version of the Bible.

Scripture quotations marked NKJV™ are taken from the New King James Version®. Copyright © 1982 by Thomas Nelson, Inc. Used by permission. All rights reserved.

Hymn texts with the abbreviation *LSB* are from *Lutheran Service Book*, copyright © 2006 Concordia Publishing House. All rights reserved.

This publication may be available in Braille, in large print, or on cassette tape for the visually impaired. Please allow 8 to 12 weeks for delivery. Write to Lutheran Braille Workers, P.O. Box 5000, Yucaipa, CA 92399; call toll-free 1-800-925-6092; or visit the Web site: www.LBWinc.org.

Manufactured in the United States of America

1 2 3 4 5 6 7 8 9 10 22 21 20 19 18 17 16 15 14 13

Contents

Introduction

Welcome to LifeLight

A special pleasure is in store for you. You will be instrumental in leading your brothers and sisters in Christ closer to Him who is our life and light (John 1:4). You will have the pleasure of seeing fellow Christians discover new insights and rediscover old ones as they open the Scriptures and dig deep into them, perhaps deeper than they have ever dug before. More than that, you will have the pleasure of sharing in this wonderful study.

LifeLight—An In-depth Study

LifeLight is a series of in-depth Bible studies. The goal of LifeLight is that through a regular program of in-depth personal and group study of Scripture, more and more Christian adults may grow in their personal faith in Jesus Christ, enjoy fellowship with the members of His body, and reach out in love to others in witness and service.

In-depth means that this Bible study includes the following four components: individual daily home study; discussion in a small group; a lecture presentation on the Scripture portion under study; and an enhancement of the week's material (through reading the enrichment magazine).

LifeLight Participants

LifeLight participants are adults who desire a deeper study of the Scriptures than is available in the typical Sunday morning adult Bible class. (Mid-to-older teens might also be LifeLight participants.) While LifeLight does not assume an existing knowledge of the Bible or special experience or skills in Bible study, it does assume a level of commitment that will bring participants to each of the nine weekly assemblies having read the assigned readings and attempted to answer the study questions. Daily reading and study will require from 15 to 30 minutes for the five days preceding the LifeLight assembly. The day following the assembly will be spent reviewing the previous week's study by going over the completed study leaflet and the enrichment magazine.

LifeLight Leadership

While the in-depth process used by LifeLight begins with individual study and cannot achieve its aims without this individual effort, it cannot be completed by individual study alone. Therefore, trained leaders are necessary. You fill one or perhaps more of the important roles described below.

The Director

This person oversees the LifeLight program in a local center (which may be a congregation or a center operated by several neighboring congregations). The director

- serves as the parish LifeLight overall coordinator and leader;
- coordinates the scheduling of the LifeLight program;
- orders materials;
- convenes LifeLight leadership-team meetings;
- develops publicity materials;
- recruits participants;
- maintains records and budgeting;
- assigns, with the leadership team, participants to small discussion groups;
- makes arrangements for facilities;
- communicates outreach opportunities to small-group leaders and to congregational boards;
- follows up on participants who leave the program.

The Assistant Director *(optional)*

This person may assist the director. Duties listed for the director may be assigned to the assistant director as mutually agreeable.

The Lecture Leader

This person prepares and delivers the lecture at the weekly assembly. **(Lesson material for the lecture leader begins on p. 9.)** The lecture leader

- prepares and presents the Bible study lecture to the large group;
- prepares worship activities (devotional thought,

hymn, prayer), using resources in the study leaflet and leaders guide and possibly other, outside sources;

- helps the small-group discussion leaders to grow in understanding the content of the lessons;
- encourages prayer at weekly leadership-team and discussion-leaders meetings.

The Small-Group Coordinator *(optional; the director may fill this role)*

This person supervises and coordinates the work of the small-group discussion leaders. The small-group coordinator

- recruits with the leadership-team the small-group discussion leaders;
- trains or arranges for training of the discussion leaders;
- assists the director and discussion leaders in follow-up and outreach;
- encourages the discussion leaders to contact absent group members;
- participates in the weekly leadership-team and discussion-leaders equipping meetings;
- provides ongoing training and support as needed.

The Small-Group Discussion Leaders

These people guide and facilitate discussion of LifeLight participants in the small groups. **(Lesson material for the small-group leaders begins on p. 57.)** There should be one discussion leader for every group of no more than twelve participants. The small-group discussion leaders are, perhaps, those individuals who are most important to the success of the program. They should, therefore, be chosen with special care and be equipped with skills needed to guide discussion and to foster a caring fellowship within the group. These discussion leaders

- prepare each week for the small-group discussion by using the study leaflet and small-group leaders guide section for that session;
- read the enrichment magazine as a study supplement;
- guide and facilitate discussion in their small group;
- encourage and assist the discussion group in prayer;
- foster fellowship and mutual care within the discussion group;
- attend weekly discussion-leaders training meetings.

Leadership Training

LifeLight leaders will meet weekly to review the previous week's work and plan the coming week. At this session, leaders can address concerns and prepare for the coming session. LifeLight is a 1½-hour program with no possibility for it to be taught in the one hour typically available on Sunday mornings. Some congregations, however, may want to use the Sunday morning Bible study hour for LifeLight preparation and leadership training. In such a meeting, the lecture leader and/or small-group coordinator may lead the discussion leaders through the coming week's lesson, reserving 5 or 10 minutes for problem solving or other group concerns.

While it requires intense effort, LifeLight has proven to bring great benefit to LifeLight participants. The effort put into this program, both by leaders and by participants, will be rewarding and profitable.

The LifeLight Weekly Schedule

Here is how LifeLight will work week by week:

1. Before session 1, each participant will receive the study leaflet for session 1 and the enrichment magazine for the course. The study leaflet contains worship resources (for use both in individual daily study and at the opening of the following week's assembly) and readings and study questions for five days. Challenge questions will lead those participants who have the time and desire a greater challenge into even deeper levels of study.

2. After the five days of individual study at home, participants will gather for a weekly assembly of all LifeLight participants. The assembly will begin with a brief period of worship (5 minutes). Participants will then join their assigned small discussion groups (of twelve or fewer, which will remain the same throughout the course), where they will go over the week's study questions together (55 minutes). Assembling together once again, participants will listen to a lecture presentation on the readings they have studied in the previous week and discussed in their small groups (20 minutes). After the lecture presentation, the director or another leader will distribute the study leaflet for the following week. Closing announcements and other necessary business may take another five minutes before dismissal.

In some places some small groups will not join the weekly assembly because of scheduling or other reasons. Such groups may meet at another time and place (perhaps in the home of one of the small group's members). Those congregations may record the lecture given by the lecture leader at the weekly assembly and duplicate it for use by other groups meeting later in the week.

3. On the day following the assembly, participants will review the preceding week's work by rereading the study leaflet they completed (and that they perhaps supplemented or corrected during the discussion in their small group) and by reading appropriate articles in the enrichment magazine.

Then the LifeLight weekly study process will begin all over again!

Recommended Study Resources and Worship

The Lutheran Study Bible. St. Louis: Concordia Publishing House, 2009. This resource contains more than 26,000 study and application notes, a most thorough reference guide (pp. lxv–cx), and over 90,000 cross-references, as well as a 31,000-entry concordance, maps, charts, and timelines.

Roehrs, Walter R., and Martin H. Franzmann. *Concordia Self-Study Commentary.* St. Louis: Concordia Publishing House, 1979. This one-volume commentary on the Bible contains 950 pages and is tailored for lay use.

The Concordia Organist is a 31-CD collection of pipe organ accompaniments for all the hymns and liturgical music in *Lutheran Service Book*. St. Louis: Concordia Publishing House (order no.99-2264). Use these CDs for worship hymn accompaniment.

A New Start and a Coming Savior

Selected Passages

Preparing for the Session

Central Focus

The last three books of the Old Testament reflect upon the final phase of God's holy nation prior to the arrival of Jesus Christ. Before we delve into the books themselves, we will review what was going on in Israel during and after the Babylonian exile. Then we will have a better context within which to hear the prophets' inspired messages for our day as well.

Objectives

That participants, led by the Holy Spirit working through God's Word, will

1. identify where the exile fits into the history of the Old Testament;
2. recall the special role that the Lord gave to the prophets who spoke in His name; and
3. take note where the prophetic Scriptures reveal Christ's person and work.

Note for the small-group leaders: Lesson notes and other materials you will need begin on page 57.

For the Lecture Leader

Session Plan

Worship

Begin the session with the hymn printed in the study leaflet. Accompaniments are available in denominational hymnals, such as *Lutheran Service Book* or *Lutheran Worship* (refer to hymnal index). (Note: Concordia Publishing House has available *The Concordia Organist*. All the initial worship hymns in the LifeLight courses are included in this resource. It's especially helpful for mission congregations and small parishes. See the list of study resources on p. 7.) Follow with this prayer:

Prayer

Almighty God, Creator of heaven and earth, open our minds and hearts by the power of Your Holy Spirit, so that we may read Your Word and believe in what You have done for us in Jesus Christ, Your dear Son. When You brought Your chosen people back from their time of exile, You renewed Your precious promises to them and pointed their faith toward the coming Savior of the world. Through that same Word of truth, purify Your Church on earth, distinguish it from the evils of this world, and let Your mercy shine upon us in forgiveness until we come to that eternal life that You have prepared for us in Christ, for it is in His name we pray. Amen.

Lecture Presentation

Introduction

The Books of Haggai, Zechariah, and Malachi, found in the back of the Old Testament, were written after the people of Judah returned from the Babylonian captivity. Before we begin delving deeply into the riches contained in these three books of the prophets, let's spend some time in a broad overview of our topic. Today, we will review the history of the Babylonian captivity and the temple in Jerusalem. Then, we will briefly look at the prophets and their visions and prophecies. Finally, we will conclude with a short sketch of how salvation history continued from the close of the Book of Malachi to the opening of the Book of Matthew.

1 Exile and Return (2 Chronicles 36:15–23; Leviticus 26:27–45; Jeremiah 25:1–14)

Unlike the captivity in Egypt that God's people went through before the exodus, this was a forced expulsion from the Promised Land—a direct consequence of idolatry on the part of God's people. It wasn't that God was especially touchy about this one particular commandment over all the others. He alone could see that the hearts of His chosen ones were stone-cold toward Him. They rejected His grace and refused to believe His promises. They even laughed at His threats of punishment. Spiritually, their faith was choked by the weeds of man-made gods they had allowed to spring up around them.

Therefore, after generations of warnings issued through prophet after prophet, the Lord finally called upon foreign conquerors to overthrow His divided people.

The Northern Kingdom, which retained the name Israel, was composed of ten tribes that had separated from the other two in the south, namely Judah and Benjamin (1 Kings 12), and established a rival capital in the city of Samaria, less than fifty miles north of Jerusalem. For their entire history as a separate nation, they declared themselves independent from the true worship of God. Because of this hardened and determined rejection of Him, the Lord raised up the kingdom of Assyria to swoop in, destroy Samaria and the surrounding cities, and force all the inhabitants away like scattered sheep. Some foreigners were brought in to resettle the area surrounding the destroyed city, mixing their pagan religions with the worship of the one true God. This gave rise to a despised culture of people who would later be called the Samaritans.

The Southern Kingdom, called Judah, merely delayed the inevitable. About 130 years after Samaria fell to the Assyrians, King Nebuchadnezzar of Babylon laid siege to Jerusalem and eventually destroyed the Holy City, including the precious temple building that Solomon had dedicated to the name of the Lord. By the end of the siege and the fall of Jerusalem, most of the people had been taken into exile, and all the wealth of the land had been either destroyed or plundered. Jeremiah was in the middle of the whole ordeal, and he is likely the mournful author of Lamentations. Just as God had threatened, the Judahites, who later came to be known as "Jews," would be banished from the Promised Land for seventy years. Most would never return to their homeland.

Then, as God Himself directed the events of history, Persia rose to dominate the Middle Eastern world, and King Cyrus came to power over the lands once dominated by Assyria and Babylonia. It was Cyrus who issued the surprising and earth-shattering decree that allowed the worshipers of the Lord to rebuild His temple in Jerusalem. Thousands had been shipped out, but only hundreds returned to settle in the lands of their fathers. Things were not going to be the same as they had been for their ancestors. The temple would have none of the magnificent splendor that Solomon had given it. The people were often discouraged, because it was a difficult task to reinstitute the Lord's form of worship and government among themselves. The priests were not moving back in sufficient numbers to do their specific jobs. The temple building project was delayed, at times almost sabotaged. People were more concerned with building their own houses. Some men divorced their legitimate wives and married foreign women who refused to give up their pagan religions. There were no more kings sitting on the throne to rule in this brave, renewed world. Everything seemed to be starting over from scratch.

As the returned exiles faced these new challenges and frustrations, they needed a new generation of prophets to call them to repentance and spur them on to the Lord's plan for His people. The last three of the Minor Prophets, namely Haggai, Zechariah, and Malachi, were the men whom God called to speak that encouraging Word. The exile was over, but the Lord was not done with His saving work. These three prophets would preach God's answer to the question "We're back . . . so what now?"

2 Oracles and Burdens (Ezekiel 33:7–9)

The Book of Hebrews begins, (1:1) "Long ago, at many times and in many ways, God spoke to our fathers by the prophets." For centuries, divine words were spoken through human mouths. Prophets were usually not the public worship leaders of God's people, as Samuel had been. A few of them were women, such as Huldah (2 Kings 22). Some saw visions (Isaiah), some sang divinely inspired songs (Jeremiah, Miriam, David), while others just repeated what they were told. Some were occasionally required to act out the message that God had given them (Hosea and Ezekiel, for instance). Not all of them were commanded to produce books of prophecy. Some would write, others would just speak, and still others would run away (like Jonah)!

But one thing that all the prophets shared was that they were specifically sent by the Lord to deliver a certain message from Him. Whatever their particular prophetic mandate was, they were granted unique authority to speak as though God Himself were doing the talking. In the Hebrew language, someone who was entrusted with giving a message or completing a transaction on behalf of another was called a *shaliach* (shah-LEE-ock), or "someone sent." Today, we would see that kind of authority vested in an ambassador, one who speaks or acts on behalf of his or her country's government. A *shaliach* was not given a blank check, as it were, as though he could claim that *everything* from his mouth was God's Word. Instead, hearers were required to honor a prophet's authority only when he passed on the Lord's own words. Not all the prophets actually received the honor that was due to a *shaliach*—for instance, Jeremiah was cast into an empty cistern because of an unpopular message—yet the Lord still brought about what He had instructed the prophet to say in His name.

In order to make the message absolutely clear to their hearers, prophets often adopted certain phrases that emphasized that what they were saying or writing down was in fact God's Word. Sometimes the oracle, or divine saying, was prefaced with the formula "Thus says the Lord." This attached the holy name of God, "Yahweh," to His Word that had established a covenant with His people. Many times, the prophecy concluded with the words "declares the Lord," a phrase that confessed the same truth. Occasionally when some prophets faced opposition because they were bearers of bad news, their announcement of forthcoming punishment was referred to as the "burden of the Lord." Faithful prophets cannot do anything other than pass along God's Word for the benefit of His people. Paul echoes this in the New Testament when he writes, (1 Corinthians 9:16) "For necessity is laid upon me. Woe to me if I do not preach the gospel!"

Faithful hearers also had a duty to listen and even judge the words that a prophet spoke to them. Moses gave the children of Israel certain criteria to follow as they evaluated a prophetic message. The simple rule was this: (Deuteronomy 18:22) "When a prophet speaks in the name of the Lord, if the word does not come to pass or come true, that is a word that the Lord has not spoken; the prophet has spoken it presumptuously. You need not be afraid of him." While it is true that most of what the prophets had to say was about some event in the future, they also called for faith to flourish in the hearts of their hearers from that point onward. It wouldn't have made sense for a prophet to predict the coming of a great event of salvation or destruction, and then say, "But you can do whatever you want until then!" Repentance and faithfulness to the Lord were always the goal and common themes of the prophets who truly spoke in God's name, since their overall role was to point to Jesus.

3 Focus on the Temple (1 Kings 8:22–30)

The Old Testament temple was the place where God dwelt on earth among His people and for the benefit of His people. The temple was the gathering point for them to receive His grace during the prescribed festivals and ritual sacrifices. It was the focal point of Old Testament worship. However, it had been destroyed by the Babylonians. Following the Babylonian captivity, the Israelites knew that their first major task would be to rebuild the temple. We can briefly recall what the Scriptures tell us about both the temple that had been destroyed and the tabernacle that preceded it.

The Lord's first house of worship was a tent pitched out in the Sinai wilderness. It was designed according to His own detailed specifications, which He handed down to Moses after the Israelites were liberated from Egypt. Whenever this massive, moving nation vacated a site, the priests and their assistants, the Levites, had to work carefully to dissemble and transport the tabernacle and its precious contents. The pillar of cloud and fire that led them during their times of journey remained stationary over the tabernacle during the times they were told to stay put. Even after Joshua led the people across the Jordan River into the Promised Land, the tabernacle continued as the place where God met with man.

The idea for a permanent temple seems to have come from King David. In 2 Samuel 7 (repeated in 1 Chronicles 17), David had just brought in the ark to Jerusalem, his new capital city. When the humble-looking tent was pitched near the magnificent royal palace, the king couldn't avoid the thought that the Lord needed to be treated with greater honor than that. Even though God was greatly pleased with David, and He promised that the future Messiah would come from his kingly line, He nevertheless gave the privilege to Solomon instead to build a replacement for the tabernacle.

And build it he did! Solomon spent seven years constructing a crown jewel on the top of Mount Moriah, assembling cedar, stone, and mind-boggling amounts of gold to serve as the Lord's glorious house of worship. Solomon's prayer sounds humble: (1 Kings 8:27) "Behold, heaven and the highest heaven cannot contain You; how much less this house that I have built!" Yet it was never God's objective merely to be contained in a place on earth, but rather He desired to allow His name, that is, His mighty power of salvation for His people, to become graciously and permanently accessible. The temple would bear witness to the Lord's promise to hear His peoples' prayers and one day send His Son in the flesh to make the once-for-all sacrifice for sin. To the Hebrew worshipers climbing up the hill, preparing to celebrate a festival unto the Lord, the temple was an object of pride and devotion.

All attention was given to the temple not only when it was built and dedicated, but also approximately 370 years later when it was destroyed. The Babylonians left nothing of the former edifice, and God's people began to question whether He would ever again have mercy on them. Will He ever hear our prayers? Daniel seemed to hold out hope for a rebuilt temple—for even while living in the land of exile, even at the risk of the lions' den, he prayed at his window that looked out toward Jerusalem. Perhaps there were many other Israelites who shared that same hope.

Interest in the temple sprang to new life when Cyrus came to power and decreed that the Israelite exiles could return to Jerusalem and rebuild the house of the Lord. The man who would take up the project and inspire the once-exiled people of God was a royal descendant of David and Solomon named Zerubbabel. He was not a king, nor would he be made into a king. The Persian Empire allowed him to serve as governor of the province of Judea, and it provided him with the necessary resources to commence work on the temple. Thanks to the spiritual help of dedicated servants of the Lord such as Ezra, Joshua the high priest, Haggai, and Zechariah, the second temple was completed seventy years after the Babylonians destroyed the first one, just as Jeremiah had predicted.

The focus on the holiness of God's dwelling place would continue in succeeding centuries, because Zerubbabel's temple was small and plain in comparison with the one Solomon had built. The temple was no longer a beautiful trophy high on Jerusalem's skyline. Apathy was tearing many people away from their God. Yet the faithful layman Nehemiah knew that no matter what the building looked like, the Lord's name and promised blessing was still there. Finally, the prophet Malachi was the last in a line of faithful preachers to point forward to the coming Savior, the One who would "suddenly come to His temple" (3:1) and purify all who approach Him in faith. Until there came Jesus, however, this building would be the means by which man could access God's forgiveness. That is why the prophets paid such close attention to the temple.

4 Looking toward the End (Isaiah 65:17–25; Matthew 25:31–46)

As we will also see in some of the later sessions of our Bible study, the prophets were given visions of the end times. Even before the Babylonian exile, the Lord was revealing His plan to rescue all believers for all eternity. Isaiah wrote down his prophecies about a century before the temple was destroyed, but he was still inspired to include God's promise of new heavens and a new earth (ch. 65). Jeremiah was seeing the end as already inaugurated with the coming of the Christ when he reported: (31:31, 34) "Behold, the days are coming, declares the LORD, when I will make a new covenant. . . . And no longer shall each one teach his neighbor and each his brother, saying, 'Know the LORD,' for they shall all know Me." At the beginning of the exile, prophets like Ezekiel and Daniel were far away from home; nevertheless, they saw wonderful visions of God's glory and spoke of final spiritual battles and the Last Judgment.

After the Holy Land was resettled and the temple rebuilt, the faithful renewed their hope for the coming of the Messiah and the new, golden age of salvation that would come with Him. Patience proved to be difficult to maintain, however, because by the time Jesus did actually walk among His people, He had to inform them that (John 18:36) "My kingdom is not of this world." Even though He was rightfully called King of the Jews, believers still had to obey their secular leaders, who were appointed to be the Lord's servants. It is a similar idea as when someone receives the forgiveness of sins and is truly pure in God's sight, yet at the same time remains a sinner who struggles against the flesh until death and the advent of the New Creation. You are already a citizen of God's realm of heaven, while at the same time patiently waiting for Him to come and take you to Himself (see John 14:3).

In order to illustrate the hidden reality of this magnificent promise of eternal life and peace, the Lord chose to open the eyes of some prophets and uncover the deep truths of salvation. This special work of the Holy Spirit yields a special type of biblical literature known as the "apocalyptic" genre, from the Greek word for something "uncovered" or "revealed." The apocalyptic book that we typically think of when we hear that description is Revelation. God sees all things—past, present and future—as one and the same, so He is lending that unique perspective to human eyes when He reveals His wondrous plan in this unforgettable way. Symbols play a significant role in apocalyptic literature because they reveal further details of the inspired message. Often, they utilize images that related to the temple and the sacrificial system. Even though only Zechariah records instances of apocalyptic visions, all three of the prophets that we will study have at least something to tell us about the Lord's promises that will fully come true at the end of time.

5 The Time between the Testaments (Daniel 7:13–27; 8:19–26)

After Malachi abruptly ends his book of prophecy, there is a silence that is equally abrupt and that spans the time between the Old and New Testaments, a period of about four hundred years. Once the biblical record resumes with the Gospels, we can wonder at all the changes that have taken place. So much is different! Persia is no longer the dominant power, prophets are no longer receiving visions, and even the temple has been changed. What has happened? Is God no longer at work among His people? This gap between the Old and New Testaments can make us wish that the Book of Malachi did not end so abruptly.

But even though recorded prophetic activity came to a standstill during that time, the events through which God was preparing the world for the coming of the Savior were hurrying along at a feverish pace. Greece conquered the Persian Empire, thanks to key naval victories in the Mediterranean Sea and the widespread land domination of Alexander the Great. Because of him, the Greek language and culture made it possible for God's Word to expand well beyond Jerusalem. Successors to Alexander wrestled with one another for control of Judea and its surroundings. Then eventually the Roman Empire took over, and its extensive system of roads facilitated travel for apostles such as Paul, who started churches as they went on various missionary journeys.

No matter who was in power at the time, Jerusalem continuously remained a focus of political activity. Even though the Holy City was far removed from the nerve center of the various empires that controlled them, it still lay on an important trade route in the Middle East, and so it made sense to continue a strong presence in this city high up on a hill. Tensions rose when Greek regents started outlawing the Jewish religion and persecuting anyone who worshiped in the Jerusalem temple. The notorious ruler Antiochus IV Epiphanes defiled Zerubbabel's temple in 167 BC when he ordered a pig to be sacrificed to Zeus on the holy altar, an action that gave rise to the Maccabean Revolt. Judas Maccabeus led troops to beat back their tormentors and retake the city of Jerusalem. The rededication of the temple was remembered as the Festival of Hanukkah, or "Feast of Dedication" as it is referred to in John 10.

When King Herod the Great was granted power over Judea by Caesar Augustus, he wanted to gain favor with the Jews with a single building project that was sure to do the trick. He financed a massive remodel of the Jerusalem temple that took more than forty-six years to complete (John 2:20). The huge stones and beautiful, vaulted buildings of the new complex were a welcome sight to Judeans whose great-grandfathers had groaned at the puny, plain structure that had been built by Zerubbabel.

These four hundred years following Malachi may have been "silent" when it came to written biblical prophecy, but this was still quite an active period in Israel's history. All of a sudden, by the New Testament times, we have Pharisees, Sadducees, Zealots, Samaritans, the Sanhedrin, and rabbis, all of whom would have an impact in some way or another on the coming era. Quite a lot was going on between Malachi and Matthew!

Conclusion

The Books of Haggai, Zechariah, and Malachi have been grouped together at the end of the Minor Prophets because they all prophesied after God's people returned from exile. These men share in common with one another the task of addressing Israel in a rebuilding period, in which the faithful are found struggling to live according to their true identity. As you study these relatively short books, pay attention to two great themes: a fresh start and a coming Savior.

Concluding Activities

Conclude the session with an appropriate prayer and distribute the study leaflet for week 2.

New Temple, New Challenges

Haggai 1

Preparing for the Session

Central Focus

The prophet Haggai centers in on the largest, most obvious visible indicator of Israel's post-exile spiritual slump: the temple lying in disrepair. Until the Lord's chosen dwelling place is back in operation, He will not act according to His desire or promise for His people. God's blessings and man's sinful, unbelieving rejection of those blessings quite simply cannot coexist.

Objectives

That participants, led by the Holy Spirit working through God's Word, will

1. identify the chief spiritual problem that Haggai was called to address;
2. relate the prophet's words to our own distractions from God's highest blessings; and
3. draw encouragement from the Lord's grace shown to His ransomed people.

Note for the small-group leaders: Lesson notes and other materials you will need begin on page 61.

For the Lecture Leader

Session Plan

Worship

Begin the session with the hymn printed in the study leaflet. Accompaniments are available in denominational hymnals, such as *Lutheran Service Book* or *Lutheran Worship* (refer to hymnal index). (Note: Concordia Publishing House has available *The Concordia Organist.* All the initial worship hymns in the LifeLight courses are included in this resource. It's especially helpful for mission congregations and small parishes. See the list of study resources on p. 7.) Follow with this prayer:

Prayer

Almighty God, who is greater than the highest heavens yet is still pleased to dwell with us on earth, forgive us when we take Your abundant mercy for granted. Impress upon us a renewed sense of Your grace to us in Christ, our Savior, so that we may always come before You with grateful hearts and consecrated minds. Let nothing distract us from true devotion to You, and lead us to receive all Your blessings with a proper perspective, knowing that our true home is being prepared for us with You in heaven. Amen.

Lecture Presentation

1 The Time Is Not Yet (Haggai 1:1–2)

Procrastination. Putting off until tomorrow what you can do today. It's the easiest thing to begin and the toughest thing to stop. And the Lord, the God of Israel, is not going to look the other way when His people procrastinate in spiritual matters. He who knows the thoughts of all men's hearts is fully aware that the effort to rebuild His holy house is unnecessarily delayed. The returned Israelite exiles could have creatively come up with a litany of reasons to keep themselves from getting started on their religious duty, now that they were residents once again in and around the city of Jerusalem. They resigned themselves, however, to justify their delay based on a reason that ran the risk of doing maximum damage to their personal faith and to the future of Israel's hope in the promised Savior and Messiah.

Their reason was simple: it was not yet the time to build. They felt they would be downright foolish to start ahead of time. Something else needed to happen first. What that was, I'm not sure even they knew. But the excuse was a convenient way to clear the conscience, and it's an all-too-easy way to ignore God's Word. Declaring that the time to build is not yet means that you are taking the place of God, that you are deciding His holy will for Him. The Lord can see the hearts of His people. He knows that they are making something else into their god. They are turning a blind eye to the first and greatest commandment, namely, (Exodus 20:3) "You shall have no other gods before Me."

As we saw in last week's introduction, having the temple rebuilt was essential to a reestablished Israel and the prophetic expectation of the Messiah's coming. God Himself directed them to build it, and now was the time. Suppose that Moses, while God's people were still back in Egypt, had said, "Nah, I think I'll wait before I get this Passover meal going. Let's repeat a few of those other nine plagues before we move on to the angel of death." You don't suppose that the Lord would be pleased with that attitude, would He? It would be the same roughly nine hundred years later when the seventy-year Babylonian exile was complete and the nation of Israel had once again regained its freedom.

What's stopping you, folks? The Persian conqueror Cyrus had already pledged the help of his empire to get the Jerusalem temple rebuilt. Finances were also being provided through free-will offerings, as Ezra recorded in his book. The new foundation had been laid amid a mixed cry of celebration and lamentation (Ezra 3:12–13). Those outsiders, the Samaritans, wanted to sabotage the temple project by infiltrating the ranks and corrupting the worship to include their false ideas along with the true worship, but the leaders successfully fended them off. You see, the Lord had already provided an adequate answer to every legitimate excuse to delay building prior to Haggai's appearance to the scene. Now, in this post-exile time, God's people had resorted to saying simply, "The time is not yet," so the Lord sent His holy prophet Haggai to the Holy Land with the burden of a holy message.

Haggai was directed to deliver God's stern warning to all Israelites, but the first ones who needed to listen to it were the leaders, Zerubbabel and Joshua. Zerubbabel was the governor, the one who led the province of Judah with the permission of the Persian ruler. In the Scripture books of this era in history, Zerubbabel is often paired with Joshua, the high priest, the one who would have been designated to direct the all-important sacrifices and other aspects of their worship life. These two leaders needed to be called to account, because in the fifteen years after the foundation was laid (from 535 to 520 BC), there was no further progress on the building project. Whether or not they were responsible for promoting this "not yet" excuse, God has now most certainly called upon these two men to overcome it.

2 Refusing to Receive (Haggai 1:3–6)

King David would have been mortified to see what became of this later generation of his kingdom! These people who had been dedicated to the name of the Lord finally returned from their exile in a faraway land and then, in utter selfishness, they built their own houses, paneled with exquisite cedar woodwork, and shamelessly left the temple in a complete shambles! How different it had been nearly five hundred years before with the shepherd boy who had been made ruler and successor to Saul. After David was given rest from all the battles he had fought to secure and extend the borders of Israel, he was troubled at the disparity that he clearly perceived between his luxurious living quarters and the tired old tent made of animal skins and cloth that had been used for centuries as the place to meet God. And until the Lord specifically revealed a plan for David that would far outshine a physical building, even Nathan the prophet was willing to give his blessing.

It was indeed quite a contrast. David wanted to build a more suitable house for the worship of the almighty God. However, God did not allow him to do so, as a sign of the greater One to come—Jesus. Upon the return of the Israelites from exile, God ordered them to rebuild His house as a witness of His presence and the persistence of His promise to send a Savior, but the people refused. Though it would seem on the surface that the Lord had changed His mind concerning the temple—at one time He refused to let it be built, and then at another time He ordered the people to build it—in fact, the common thread was that all attention had to remain on the promised coming of Christ. Whether they had the benefit of an impressive building adorned with awe-inspiring stones (Luke 21:5) or not, what really mattered was a faith in their heart that was properly centered on their one and only Redeemer.

In Haggai's day, that faith was faltering, and the indicators of this poor spiritual condition were everywhere: after all the effort that they had expended on their farms, the harvest remained puny; they ate, but were never satisfied; drank, but were not content; were clothed, but were never warm; saved up every penny, but the stash bag was full of holes! Was God punishing them by sending scarcity and want? Or was it rather that they had blinded themselves to the true blessings that their heavenly Father had in store for them? Had they really refused to receive God's blessing?

The words of Haggai urge repentance: "Consider your ways." These words apply to us just as much as they did to the people of ancient Judah. Measure up what you've been doing lately in light of God's commandments. Turn around while you still have the opportunity. God doesn't want your meager works, and much less does He tolerate a feigned piety. What Israel's God hungers for is a heart of faith and trust in Him for all things. The works are meant for your neighbor's benefit, not God's, and not your own. What Jesus did for you in His life, death, and resurrection was all-sufficient for your salvation. Yet, He has planted the Holy Spirit in you to create a new heart, complete with a sincere desire to love and serve the Lord in the very people whom He has placed in your path, so to speak. Where you have not measured up and your ways have stumbled over your own selfishness and sin, confess to Him, and be most assuredly forgiven. Even though His people neglect Him at times, our God is ever-near and ready to bestow His temporal and spiritual blessings in abundance!

3 Demanding Blessing Where It Is Not Given (Haggai 1:7–11)

A second time the Lord of Hosts declared His message to the people through the mouth of Haggai: "Consider your ways." And a second time, this message applies to us just as much as to the people then. Repetition certainly emphasizes a point, and the Hebrew language is no exception to that rule, but besides that, the reappearance of this phrase in verse 7 highlights a further step in the process of repentance. Saying it the first time was meant to lay down the hammer of the divine Law in order to reveal the sin and its harmful effects. Then, once the believer acknowledges his or her sin and with a contrite heart confesses the transgression to the Lord, the proper fruits of repentance can be called forth from a purified heart.

In fact, the phrase translated "consider your ways" is literally "set your heart upon your paths (that you walk)." Only the noun "heart" is in the singular; the rest of the sentence is written in the plural. Now that sin had been pointed out and the mercy of the Lord had washed it away by the merits of the promised Christ, God called upon Haggai to guide the Israelite congregation as a unified whole, with one "heart" renewed by grace to do God's will, to proceed in the path that had been illuminated for them in His Word. No longer was the Lord chastising or punishing; much less was He here laying out a method of atonement as if the people could pay the price for their own sin. Rather, He was granting the guidance of the Holy Spirit and offering the promise of His good pleasure that He bestows on all who believe in Him.

The Lord was asking for repairs to the temple building, not because He wanted to keep up with the "Joneses" of some divine variety, but because He desired a stronger faith in His chosen people. He wanted to bind their faith to the specific location of His good pleasure. Faith is nothing if it does not hold on to God's forgiveness given to us in Christ. Sure, Solomon ordered imported cedar from Lebanon and overlaid everything inside and out with gold. But an impressive edifice, by itself, does not make a temple. That's why Haggai relayed the divine command simply to use local resources this time around: (v. 8) "Go up to the hills and bring wood and build the house, that I may take pleasure in it and that I may be glorified." What mattered was a faithful response to the Lord's rich grace, not a lavish display that only calls attention to man. This isn't to say that a church building should not be made to look pleasant, but whatever form it takes ought to be a proper expression of faith and love toward God, as well as a fitting gratitude for His precious gifts.

As we have previously studied about the temple, however, there was something more going on with rebuilding this particular structure than simply showing thankfulness to God. At this critical juncture in the nation's history following the exile, there was not merely a problem with Israel's priorities. Every day that went by with the temple not up and running was a day without the Lord's specifically chosen means of grace. It would be like a Christian congregation whose members had constant feasts that included all-you-could-eat bread and bottomless casks of wine, while at the same time claiming that there is no money in the budget to purchase the elements for Holy Communion! There was simply no excuse for the people to drag their feet and say that the time to build was not yet. They needed to be told that, in procrastinating the building of the temple, they were saying no to grace itself. And the Lord of hosts was warning them of that very thing. The people were looking for blessing, but not to God. They looked for much and—because they looked where God did not promise—it came to little, and when they brought it home, He blew it away. That was what would get their attention!

4 Presence and Repentance (Haggai 1:12–13)

The Israelite exiles, together with their leaders, listened to God's voice and heeded His Word. What the Lord desired first and most of all was faith in the hearts of His people, and the Word He spoke to them through His prophet accomplished that magnificent miracle. Certainly, they "obeyed" His command and got back to work on the temple rebuilding project, but since the problem was more than laziness or even selfishness, so also the solution required a renewal of the heart.

The apostle Paul wrote these well-known words: (Romans 10:17) "Faith comes from hearing, and hearing through the word of Christ." Haggai's record of the peoples' response documents this very truth. Sinners cannot ever act in obedience to the Lord who created them, unless they first hear the Word that forgives their sins. By means of that Word, believers receive the saving faith in their hearts that will then lead them to the actions that are the proper fruits of that faith. So before the prophet goes into detail on how the building project finally proceeded, he takes a moment to give credit to the Lord who got the ball rolling in the first place.

It seems that whenever a preacher has it in mind to call attention to the power of God's Word alone to accomplish His will, he runs the risk of being misunderstood and the hearers imagine that the preacher is out to magnify himself over against the congregation who is listening to him. It is feared that he is only saying, "This is the Word of the Lord," so that *whatever* he says is obeyed without question. Certainly, it takes a significant dose of humility at all times in order for clergy to alleviate this concern of the laity. Pastors can often feel the pressure to lead their flocks with tools that seem to be more effective than mere teaching and preaching God's Word. Yet the prophet's record of the Lord's mighty work of faith in the hearts of Israel's leaders and people helps us keep our priorities straight. Haggai was not given the role of vision casting or strategic planning. Israel already had leaders whom God Himself had designated for those tasks. Haggai spoke the Word faithfully, and that would be more than enough to equip God's people with faith working itself out in love.

There are three words that Haggai used in this brief passage that call attention not to himself but to the Lord who called him. The first is "prophet." This means that Haggai was designated to speak in a specific role and at the particular times when God would choose to reveal His Word. The second is "sent." This is a verb form of *shaliach*, which we previously examined. Haggai was a kind of apostle, an ambassador who carried the same authority as the Lord whom he served, but that authority was limited to the specific mission and message that he was given. A mere man spoke the Gospel, but it was really the Lord Himself who was with the people, giving His blessing along with the promise of His presence.

The last of these three words is "messenger." Most of the time in the Bible, especially in books that are older than the Book of Haggai, the word for a messenger refers to an angel from heaven. This tells us that God's Word, the message, brings its own sanctity and heavenly nature as the messenger speaks it. The preacher does not add any self-made holiness to the Word, nor does he "dress it up" with personality. Of course, he ought not hinder the Word that he preaches with an unholy life or use the Word for His selfish advantage. Instead, as the messenger faithfully speaks the Gospel, by grace alone God grants him angelic praise, even for it to be said that his feet are beautiful (Romans 10:15)!

5 Back to Building (Haggai 1:14–15)

Here we see that Haggai continued to give all credit to the Lord for the temple project getting back on track. He "stirred up the spirit" of the two leaders, Zerubbabel and Joshua, as well as all the faithful remnant of Israel. They finally realized that there was no reason to delay building. God Himself would remove every obstacle that they had feared. At least now they were no longer in the spiritual state of mind that had led them to say, "the time is not yet." Putting it off is not on the table anymore. The Lord had stirred up their spirits, so their former stubbornness and lack of faith would be unable to paralyze them this time.

Yet we should be careful not to attribute too much to this activity of stirring up spirits, either. Recall that Ezra had reported another instance when the Lord stirred up somebody's spirit where it didn't create or strengthen faith in that person's heart. The event, of course, is recorded in Ezra 1, and this time it was Cyrus who was the object of this interesting divine activity. Even though the Persian ruler "knew not" the Lord, as Isaiah had predicted of him (44:28–45:7), Cyrus was nevertheless assigned the role to allow the exiles to return to Jerusalem and begin rebuilding the temple. In the Old Testament, God stirred up believers and unbelievers alike, but whenever this action involved His own chosen people, like what we see here in Haggai 1, it helped bring about God's gifts to Israel in worship. This stirring up may not be in itself a gift of faith that was being given, but the way was being paved for God's Word of peace to do His Work of salvation once the temple was finally complete.

The man named Darius we see here, as well as in verse 1, was in the second year of his reign as king over all Persia. He is not, however, the same Darius who was mentioned in the Book of Daniel, chapters 6, 9, and 11 (and is distinguished in that Book as "Darius the Mede"). Instead of falling for boyish appeals to vanity at the expense of throwing faithful prophets into a lions' den, this Darius actually turns out to be quite helpful to Israel. Ezra received an excellent assist from him when Israel's political enemies petitioned Darius for a stop order against them, but received from him instead a decree not to interfere with the temple *and* a demand to fully finance the project! I think Israelites and non-Israelites alike dropped their jaws when that announcement was read! Thanks in no small measure to the efforts of Darius I of Persia, the temple would finally be finished.

Conclusion

Haggai's first prophetic task was successful, by God's grace. He was called to urge the returned exiles and their leaders to repentance and get the temple rebuilding project started up again. His Law-and-Gospel message was not an example of high-flying rhetoric. He rather simply pointed out the problem, gave the people a clear-cut reason why the status quo could not continue, and laid out the concrete steps that the Lord wanted His people to follow. All the hard work, so to speak, belonged to God, because He is always the One responsible for the results.

Concluding Activities

Conclude the session with an appropriate prayer and distribute the study leaflet for week 3.

The Lord Whom You Seek

Haggai 2

Preparing for the Session

Central Focus

Haggai is not a "one-issue" prophet. The temple is finally getting rebuilt, and yet the Lord has more of His Word to place on the lips of His chosen servant. God is preparing for the dawning of the Christian Church, drawn from all the nations, founded on the death and resurrection of Christ, and sealed by the signet ring of His holy work of grace as it has been seen in the ongoing history of His people.

Objectives

That participants, led by the Holy Spirit working through God's Word, will

1. note how lack of faith was blocking the blessings that God desired to give His people;
2. discover the prophecies that Haggai recorded concerning the Church; and
3. draw encouragement for their own respective roles in the church and the world.

Note for the small-group leaders: Lesson notes and other materials you will need begin on page 65.

For the Lecture Leader

Session Plan

Worship

Begin the session with the hymn printed in the study leaflet. Accompaniments are available in denominational hymnals, such as *Lutheran Service Book* or *Lutheran Worship* (refer to hymnal index). (Note: Concordia Publishing House has available *The Concordia Organist*. All the initial worship hymns in the LifeLight courses are included in this resource. It's especially helpful for mission congregations and small parishes. See the list of study resources on p. 7.) Follow with this prayer:

Prayer

O Lord God of hosts, who comes to shake the heavens and the earth, and who has promised to fill Your house with glory, we confess that we have defiled the honor of Your Word with unholy thoughts, words, and deeds. We have selfishly kept to ourselves the gifts that truly belong to You. Do not remove Your Spirit from our midst, but strengthen and purify us so that we may serve You with true and confident faith. Form us in Your image, for we are Your signet ring that carries out Your will on earth, and through Your Church obtain for Yourself a kingdom in the name of Jesus Christ, our Lord. Amen.

Lecture Presentation

1 Strength for the Present (Haggai 2:1–5)

It was a ceremony like Israel had never seen before in its history. A new temple's foundation was being dedicated among the ruins in the city of Jerusalem. Ezra recorded the events of the great fanfare that heralded this significant moment. Priests donned their sacred vestments and blew their trumpets. Levites clashed their cymbals. Psalms were sung back and forth as the people participated in a liturgy that united them with one another, as well as with their ancestors who long ago had worshiped at the very same spot. Then, Ezra writes, the people shouted with a great shout when they praised the Lord. What a cause for celebration! The foundation for God's house had been laid once again! His people had every reason to lift up their voices. And in fact, the noise was documented to have been heard from far away (Ezra 3:10–13).

The sound was a blend of jubilation and mourning, of weeping and sadness mixed in with laughter and mirth. This was why the milestone that was being observed was unique to the historical record of God's holy nation. The weeping did not arise from nostalgia or the relief that follows a long ordeal. Sadness welled up in the eyes of those who had seen the structure that had stood there before—the new temple simply could not compare with it. The old men who were carried off into exile as children with their families, and who then had been allowed to return about fifty years later, *they* finally understood the abundant blessing of God that Israel had rejected. Ezra made sure that their shock and dismay would lead them to proper repentance over the apostasy that had led to the first temple's destruction. God was not picking on them, nor was He leaving them vulnerable to the whims of their enemies. His people needed to believe in the Lord alone, even if His house of worship was not going to appear as glorious as it had been before.

About fifteen years after this foundation-laying ceremony, Haggai stands at the same site, as reconstruction is just beginning to make some headway, and he looks around him. (Haggai 2:3) "Who is left among you?" he asks. To those who had seen the former temple, who had wept when others shouted at the foundation-laying, the prophet asks concerning the temple taking shape before them, "Is it not as nothing in your eyes?" Whether the sentiment is spoken or left unsaid, the comparison between the first and second temples cannot be shaken from the minds of the Israelites. A modern comparison would be as if Buckingham Palace were replaced by a drafty, log-cabin fort.

The shock had not yet subsided, and the discouragement of this constant reminder of the former building was starting to breed despair and apathy rather than repentance. So, like a searchlight piercing the foggy darkness, Haggai focuses the Word of the Lord into three brightly shining beams as he tells the people: Be strong! Work! Fear not! Each one of these commands not only shook them out of their paralyzing depression, but it also equipped the people to believe and act as their faithful forefathers had done so long ago. Yes, the first temple that was such a beautiful sight was gone. Nevertheless, the same gracious presence of God that dwelt in Solomon's temple would now reside with His chosen people once again for their blessing. In fact, Haggai points out, ever since the great deliverance from Egypt nearly a thousand years back, the Lord had never abandoned them, for His Holy Spirit, the Third Person of the Holy Trinity, had remained in their midst (v. 5).

2 Shaking and Glorifying (Haggai 2:6–9)

The fruit is high up in the tree, well out of the reach of your ladder. And if you don't harvest those delicious, ripe specimens, the birds and insects will beat you to the first bite! What do you do? Shake the tree! Then what happens? The fruit falls onto the extra-large tarp that you so intelligently have laid out under the green canopy, and then you fold it up with your sweet treasures tucked inside. Yes, for a while, it looks like the tree is not going to be able to take the vigorous agitation that you are putting it through. However, the fruit will come off quite easily when the perfect ripeness is achieved, and then you will be well on your way to perfectly squeezed juice or the freshest possible pie.

When you read about how God said that He would shake the nations, think about a fruit tree harvest. When the Word of the Lord comes in contact with the civilizations of sinful man, there is bound to be agitation. The two will not get along together peacefully for long. Eventually, the shaking will come when the time is fully ripe. Yet, the ensuing conflict actually serves the divine will, because, when through turmoil and difficulty, God shakes a people, the fruit He harvests will be brought into His storehouse with great rejoicing. Even if some of the believers suffer a little bruising and damage in the whole shaking process, they still are rescued from the wild birds of the evil one who are out to peck them to eternal death right where they were growing. The seemingly violent activity that was being done to the tree turns out all right in the end. Harvest-time joy makes the shaking all worthwhile!

Three times in Haggai 2, the Lord spoke of His intent to commence shaking on earth according to His holy will. When God acts with omnipotent power in the midst of the world's history, all the earth—heavens and seas as well as all the nations—will be sure to know that something big is happening! Other prophets had been inspired to link a definite message from God with an earthquake. Haggai used his divinely ordained speech not only to highlight the Lord's almighty power on display, but also to signal the coming harvest of souls. There was more going on here than God merely attracting attention through a mighty miracle.

Probably the best musical rendition of verses 6–7 is found in Handel's *Messiah*. Early on in the performance of the famous oratorio, the bass soloist stands up and literally mimics the shaking with a complex run of notes that can take anyone's breath away. The words in *Messiah's* libretto are taken almost verbatim from the King James Version of the Bible, so the singular word *desire*, as in "desire of all nations" (v. 7), is interpreted in conjunction with Malachi 3:1 to refer to the coming of Jesus Christ in the fullness of time. In the ESV, as well as other similar translations, you may notice that the noun is plural: *treasures* instead of *desire*. The Hebrew sentence looks confusing at first, because even though the noun is plural, the verb is singular, as if to say literally, "the desired things from all nations, it shall come in."

It is certainly true that when the Christ comes again, He will cause a great convulsion in all nations. And it is also true that He will inhabit His holy temple so that its glory will become greater than before. However, the Bible also speaks of the Church in this curious way: where at first, God speaks of all believers individually, but then refers to them together as one entity that will later be called the Church. In other words, "the desired things from all the nations" refers to individual Christians, and "it" (that is, the Church) shall come in.

3 Spiritual Meaning of "Unclean" (Haggai 2:10–14)

As you were reading the ritual rules governing "clean" and "unclean" in Leviticus and Numbers, was it becoming a little too difficult to follow? Did you reflect upon how fortunate you are to believe in Christ *after* His coming rather than to be an Israelite during the time *before* He came? I would have been so occupied by this or that sacrifice or festival regulation that I wouldn't have been able to concentrate on anything else! And maybe that was the point of all those ceremonial laws, after all. The whole spectrum of liturgical actions that God's people needed to perform day to day, week to week, month to month, year to year—all of it testified to God's will for His people to prepare in some way for the coming Savior. Some of the rituals described how salvation would come from the Messiah; others simply highlighted the people's utter need for His gift of grace.

In the Old Testament, what did it mean to be "unclean"? As the Lord was setting up the rituals through which He would allow His redeemed people to draw near to His holy presence, He instructed Moses to establish some boundaries. The devastating effects of sin in the fallen and corrupted world unfortunately separated creature from Creator. Lack of faith and a rejection of God's Word would hinder any attempt at reconciliation. As the promise of Christ was unfolding little by little, whatever things God chose to use to help proclaim our Savior were acceptable before His presence because of His abundant grace and forgiveness. For example, those animals that were approved for sacrifices and festivals were considered clean, and they were the means by which a believer received the favor of the Lord. Whatever testified to death and separation from our heavenly Father was considered out of bounds and rejected from God's liturgical holy places.

A person became unclean for a variety of reasons and, for a little while at least, was considered to be outside of the Israelite community. This did not necessarily mean that the person had lost his or her faith, or had done something morally wrong, or would be cut off permanently. Most of the time, the unclean person faced a certain time of separation from the rest of the people, a cleansing ritual at which a priest usually officiated, before being eventually reincorporated into the worshiping community. It would take only a few repetitions of the purification process, no doubt, before an Israelite would be sure to value his or her status as being ritually clean. The person would want to avoid becoming unclean wherever and whenever possible.

Haggai was instructed to ask the priests in Jerusalem a simple line of questions regarding an important aspect of clean versus unclean. As the ceremonial law indicates, some things, such as a garment, can be considered clean by virtue of contact with something else that is clean (cf. Lv 6:27); yet, that cleanness cannot be passed on to anything else. On the other hand, when someone is declared unclean—for instance, for touching a dead body—then that person's uncleanness can be communicated to anything else that the person touches. It's a similar principle involved when Paul said, (Galatians 5:9) "A little leaven leavens the whole lump."

This analogy that was affirmed by the priests' answers gave Haggai the perfect object lesson through which he would reveal the deeper spiritual malady that was going on among God's people. Just as an unclean person was capable of spreading uncleanness to other items, so also the lack of faith among the Israelites was spreading and hindering God's blessing from flowing to them in abundance. Other aspects of their lives were also suffering the consequences of their uncleanness. Yes, they were finally getting back to work on building the temple, but the Lord was most interested in their hearts.

Nothing clean can make other things clean; yet, there is one notable exception: our Savior, Jesus Christ. His forgiving Word and gentle touch of mercy cleanses the uncleanness of our faithlessness, and so we are reincorporated into the community upon which our Lord shines His face with peace.

4 God's Blessings Out of Nothing (Haggai 2:15–19)

Hebrew-speaking people saw themselves passing through time as though they were walking backwards. We can think of it like this: the future, toward which we are walking, is still behind us because we don't know what will happen at a later time. We proceed through our time in history by looking at the past. It is the past, not the future, that we can see and reflect upon. It is the past that we have already experienced and that still has much to teach us. A perspective like that may sound silly to us in our culture, because we are convinced that what lies ahead—even though it may be unknown—should take up our full attention. In contrast to the people of Bible times, we tend to have our backs to the past and our faces toward the future.

Yet, Haggai is true to his own worldview when he preaches to the nation of Israel: (v. 15) "Consider from this day backward." Most English Bible translations render this as "Consider from this day onward"; however, it would be more accurate to render it as "Consider from this day backward." That is to say, as you continue to walk backward toward the unknown future, recall what lessons lie right in front of your face. Learn from God's actions toward you that He has been urging you to repentance. The uncertain future behind you will be bright if you dare to put your faith in the amazing mercy of the Lord your God!

If the holy people had given appropriate attention to the many signs that were meant to wake them up spiritually, they would have been fully aware that it was God's fervent desire to bless and prosper them. He also wanted to tie that blessing directly to the temple project so that they could be assured that "every good gift and every perfect gift is from above, coming down from the Father of lights with whom there is no variation or shadow due to change" (James 1:17). As they progressed toward finishing the space that would be rededicated to the gracious dwelling of the Lord on earth, they would begin to see improvement in the resources of their land and the fruits of their labor.

What was actually happening, however, was the opposite. They lagged behind and put off their solemn duty. They had claimed that it was not yet the time for building. They pointed to a lackluster crop as tearing them away from the temple project, and then they heard that the crop situation would not be improving because the temple was not yet finished. What a vicious circle! The people demanded not only that God would provide for them out of nothing, but also that He would provide their necessities despite their disobedience to Him!

As a reaction to this demonstrated lack of faith, it was in the Lord's wisdom to bring the people to their knees: He sent them blight, mildew, and hail. The vine, fig tree, the pomegranate, and the olive tree all were bare. Nothing is ever produced without our heavenly Father granting it. Does this mean that we, too, should consider our bad times and the mishaps of our life to be a punishment from God for some lack of faith on our part? No, but if we feel the need to ask the question, then perhaps it is time for us to repent and trust in Jesus so that our faith may be strengthened. We Christians have not been given the task of preparing for the world's Savior, because He has already come. Our buildings are not divinely designed or mandated. For Christians, suffering may not be a sign that we have rejected God, but rather an occasion for rejoicing, as we read in James 1:2–3, "Count it all joy, my brothers, when you meet trials of various kinds, for you know that the testing of your faith produces steadfastness." And even if it did turn out that the adverse harvest was a divine punishment, the good news for Haggai and his congregation was that it would soon be over, thanks to the Lord's mercy. Without anything that they have done to deserve it, God made this promise: (Haggai 2:19) "From this day on I will bless you."

5 You Shall Be My Signet (Haggai 2:20–23)

The Book of Haggai began with a message from the Lord "by the hand of Haggai" that was intended for both Zerubbabel the governor and Joshua the high priest. That first word from God was locked in their present circumstances—focused on the temple that had not yet been finished. It may have been sent to those two leaders originally in written form. Now that we see the last prophetic utterance that was recorded in the book, we take note that the Lord's words were going to be spoken this time, and that they were directed only to one of those two pillars of God's holy people, namely, the descendant of King David, Zerubbabel. He was granted an encouraging prediction of what was yet to come in the promised age of the Messiah. For the first time, Haggai spoke of the future for Judah and its leaders.

It sounded like it would be a bumpy ride! Yet all the "wars and rumors of wars" that would roil the world in the centuries to come would actually serve a divine purpose. God had revealed to Haggai two months prior that He would shake the heavens and the earth. This predicted upheaval was a key ingredient in the dish He had in mind. And as the nations are shaken, their treasured fruit—that is, the believers who will be drawn from all lands—will fill the Church and glorify the Lord through faith in Jesus Christ.

Zerubbabel himself would not see the fulfillment of the events that Haggai was inspired to predict. He would oversee the completion of the second temple and preside over the province of Judah during a time of relative peace, with only minor incidents with neighboring leaders (Ezra and Nehemiah recorded these events with some detail). There would be no knock-down, drag-out, Armageddon-type battle under Zerubbabel's watch. The phrase "on that day" (v. 23) is common in the writings of many Old Testament prophets, but Haggai has it written down just once. Those important words most often refer to the events that testify to the coming of Christ.

Because Zerubbabel was a descendant of King David's royal house, he was also an ancestor in the family tree of Jesus. That is the reason why the Lord gave him a special distinction. Judah's leader at the time of the conclusion of the Babylonian exile would be known as the "signet ring" of the Lord of Hosts. It would be the pleasure of the almighty God to identify Himself with His people Israel and their anointed leader. A signet was a kind of authorized signature; it was unique to the bearer and, when used on seals and documents, it carried his full authority. The owner engraved the design of his seal on a medallion so that it would make an irreproducible impression on wax or a lump of soft clay. In order to guard against ancient-world identity theft, this signet was kept close to the owner, so that either he wore it as a ring, or he had it fastened to a cord that he wore around his neck.

Designating Zerubbabel as a signet ring of the Lord means that the promise of a Savior was going to remain alive for all believers. History would continue to march toward the Messiah's coming and the salvation He would win for the world. The faithful Israelites would, for the time being, worship in a humble re-creation of the temple, but the great day of fulfillment would make those days pale in comparison.

Conclusion

Ezra informed us that Haggai's preaching helped the returned Jewish exiles rebuild the temple in Jerusalem. We saw how he was granted the grace of God to fulfill this task. We leave the small Book of Haggai for now and turn to the other prophet who was speaking at about the same time. Zechariah will further unfold the colorful messianic tapestry on which Haggai had only started with a few stitches.

Concluding Activities

Conclude the session with an appropriate prayer and distribute the study leaflet for week 4.

Visions of Jerusalem

Zechariah 1–4

Preparing for the Session

Central Focus

The prophet Zechariah was allowed to see a series of visions through which he would proclaim the plans of the Lord that would eventually unfold not only for the Jews of his time but for all believers of all times, who will come from all nations. This work of grace would center on Jesus Christ Himself, for He is the Son of God who came to dwell with humans on earth and to remove their iniquity forever on a single day.

Objectives

That participants, led by the Holy Spirit working through God's Word, will

1. become familiar with apocalyptic passages found in Zechariah and elsewhere in Scripture;
2. link the visions to their fulfillment in the New Testament Church; and
3. receive encouragement and motivation to confess God's name to all people.

Note for the small-group leaders: Lesson notes and other materials you will need begin on page 68.

For the Lecture Leader

Session Plan

Worship

Begin the session with the hymn printed in the study leaflet. Accompaniments are available in denominational hymnals, such as *Lutheran Service Book* or *Lutheran Worship* (refer to hymnal index). (Note: Concordia Publishing House has available *The Concordia Organist*. All the initial worship hymns in the LifeLight courses are included in this resource. It's especially helpful for mission congregations and small parishes. See the list of study resources on p. 7.) Follow with this prayer:

Prayer

Protect us, merciful Father, from everything that threatens our faith in You. Without Your angels guarding us, our souls will never find rest on earth, for Satan and his forces constantly mount their attacks. But since You have gained the victory over our enemies through the blood of Jesus Christ, Your Son, we pray that our hearts may be fixed on Him as our Savior, the Branch, the One who purifies us in Baptism and plants us by pure grace into the fellowship of Your Holy Church forever. Grant that Your kingdom may come among us, not by might, nor by power, but by Your Holy Spirit, for the sake of Christ, our Lord, and all that He has done for us. Amen.

Lecture Presentation

1 Return (Zechariah 1:1–6)

When Ezra documented the temple rebuilding project, he made mention of both Haggai and Zechariah, saying that through their inspired words they supported the leaders and the Jews (Ezra 5:1–2). We have seen already how Haggai focused on the task at hand and how, in his prophetic ministry, he called the people to repentance over their fifteen-year sluggish start on this all-important building project. Zechariah, on the other hand, was inspired by the Holy Spirit to reach back further into history for a starting point. His book does not talk about the temple in the same way that Haggai's does. Yet, his message continued to support and build up the returned exiles, especially as he reminded them of their crucial role in God's plan to save the world.

God called Zechariah to be a prophet while also serving as a priest (Nehemiah 12:40–41). It would be logical to assume that he would have had every reason to urge the completion of the temple project, because he was closely involved with all of the sacrifices and feasts that were commanded in that holy space. Priests were very careful about their family lines and genealogies. They needed to trace their family tree back to Moses' brother Aaron. It was their evidence that they were indeed the legitimate servants whom God set aside to administer His means of grace for the people through the Old Testament sacrifices. Pastors today locate this sign of authentication in their call, which usually is issued by means of a congregation. It is an outward testimony to the God who alone assigns the sacred duties in the Office of the Ministry. Similarly, for a priest in the Old Testament, to be proven as descended from Aaron assured both the man and also the people he served that God's promises would be most certainly accessible to them via the hand of this particular consecrated servant.

The name Zechariah means "the Lord remembers," which was a truth about God that could cut both ways. On the one hand, the one true God was capable of remembering the past sins of His people and would urgently remind the people through Zechariah that they should not repeat the faithlessness that their fathers had engaged in prior to the Babylonian exile. The condemning words of judgment overtook them, and they had to pay the consequences. There was no fooling the Creator of the world. He was always there—and it would, of course, be impossible for Him to forget, even though the prophets themselves never lasted forever. His Word remained permanent. And the Lord would remember whenever His people strayed from Him.

On the other hand, the merciful Lord would never fail to remember His promise He had made to Abraham and all of Abraham's countless descendants who trusted in Him. In fact, He would call that promise to the remembrance of each generation as children took over the traditions handed down from their parents. God's remembering in this sense speaks primarily of actions, and not merely thoughts. Centuries before, when Noah was on the ark with his family and all those animals, he was comforted to know that God would follow through on what He said would happen. This is what is behind the idea of God "remembering" something. It is not that something had slipped His mind and now He suddenly remembered, but rather that He would never forget or disregard His promises. For example, as we read in Genesis 8:1, "But God remembered Noah" and immediately set in motion the winds that He would use to dry the floodwaters. Thanks to God's act of "remembering," the floating zoo soon came back to rest on dry land. He made it plain that His promises would come true as He said they would. Zechariah employs both forms of God's capability to remember: first when he delivers the call to return to the Lord, and then when he depicts the salvation of God's people as he saw it through eight night visions.

2 A Horseman and Scattering Horns (Zechariah 1:7–21)

Three months after the initial call to repentance, Zechariah's prophetic career took a unique turn. Most prophets, including Haggai, were given divine messages to proclaim word-for-word to the intended recipients. This time, however, the Word of the Lord would arrive in a series of dreamlike images, complete with interactive, explanatory dialogue. How's that for audiovisual media! We have immediately switched course in biblical literature from the prophetic style to the apocalyptic style. Apocalyptic portions of the Bible are those writings that point us to the Last Day and the sure and certain hope we have in Christ: the resurrection of the dead and the life of the world to come. Very often, the information in apocalyptic books is presented in the form of visions. Examples of other apocalyptic books include Daniel and Revelation.

The hidden truth suddenly revealed to Zechariah in bright, colorful pictures indicates the end of the exile and the announcement of the coming Savior. The striking similarity to John's visions that are recorded in the Book of Revelation is no accident. There is only one story of rescue for God's faithful people, even though the Holy Spirit wrote that story through many different human authors.

Zechariah saw several entities all at once in the first night vision, but he waited to write about them until he turned his attention to each one. The first to catch his inspired gaze was a man mounted upon a "red horse." The color was probably meant to refer to a dark reddish-brown, not a bright, Technicolor fuchsia! The word translated "behold" indicates the immediate happening of a God-ordained event. It calls attention to the vision as God's action from this point onward. The "glen," or low-lying valley in which the horseman is standing, is dotted with small evergreens, or myrtle trees. The beautiful, yet unimposing myrtle tree stands for God's holy people in these visions, and here they were being depicted as living in a low point in their history—not yet high and exalted on a hill.

This first horseman was an angel, a messenger who had been sent out on an urgent patrol mission with three others like him, and their horses were all different colors: one looked like the leader's mount, the other two were "sorrel" (a bright fox-red color) and white. Zechariah spoke up at this point in his experience, and suddenly we find out that another angel was standing there with him and answering his questions about the vision, explaining what was happening to the prophet. The angels on horses had just returned from the four main directions of the earth, and they were reporting back to yet another "angel" among the myrtles who had sent them, the Angel of the Lord. As we know from several other appearances in the Old Testament, the Angel of the Lord is often actually not a created angel but the Son of God Himself. Jesus, before He put on human flesh, appeared in Zechariah's vision—He is addressed and worshiped as God, yet He is also distinct from "the LORD of hosts," whom we may identify here as God the Father.

The four mounted messengers had just returned and reported that the land had finally come to rest from the seventy years of God's anger during the exile. This prompted the Angel of the Lord to plead to the Lord of Hosts for mercy, and Zechariah's angelic interpreter announces that the holy nation that had been scattered will soon be gathered together again. While God's house is being rebuilt, the Lord promises prosperity to return to Zion, the once-mighty fortress hill next to the temple upon which the exiles will settle again.

As a parallel with the four horses, Zechariah saw in his second vision four horns—again introduced with the word "behold." In the prophetic visions, horns often depict strength or power. Like the bulls of Pamplona running after crazed festival participants, other nations (like Babylon) had been summoned by the Lord to be "horns" that were meant to scatter the wayward Israelites. Yet even stronger nations, such as Persia, were symbolized by the craftsmen in Zechariah's vision that in turn cast down those horns. Yes, the nations that persecuted and scattered God's people had been accomplishing the Lord's will, yet it would also be the Lord's will, when their time had come to an end, to punish them for their own iniquity and rein them in again. Just as in Spain, the bulls may be at the beginning of the day quite fearsome and dangerous, but when the time of running is over, they never end up having the last word!

3 Measuring Jerusalem (Zechariah 2)

In the third vision of that night, Zechariah focused his attention not on an angel, but on a man some distance away who had a measuring cord in his hand. Large distances were marked off by stretching the line out and counting the lengths of the line. The man's answer to the prophet centers our gaze on the city of Jerusalem, post-Babylonian exile. It was a city still recovering from destruction. The people were just getting started with rebuilding the temple. Other dwellings were being constructed in its vicinity. Later on, Nehemiah would be sent to the Holy City to protect it with a new wall. Measuring the city's width and length would be seen as a necessary preparatory step in its renovation. So the man with the measuring line in his hand would be concerned with the earthly city's borders and limits. Protection from attack and preservation of limited resources were taken into consideration when Jerusalem's dimensions are found out.

Returning to the prophet's immediate vicinity, Zechariah's angelic guide was joined by another angel, who was carrying orders this time not for Zechariah but for his companion. The man with the cord did not need to determine limits for Jerusalem, after all. There would be no walls holding people in, because the city would overflow with people and possessions. It was to look like sprawling open country rather than a pent-up, fortressed city! There would be no need for humanly devised protection, because the Lord Himself would be a wall of fire, much as He was a pillar of fire and cloud for those Israelites whom He led out of Egypt and throughout a wilderness wandering long ago.

This vision revealed the future spiritual existence of Jerusalem, the home of all who believe in the Son of God, Christ, the Savior. The earthly Jerusalem of the fifth century BC would eventually get its wall rebuilt, and a finite number of people would live within its fixed borders. God would actually see to it Himself! But the Jerusalem about which the angel spoke in the vision was a different thing entirely. The abundance of believers who will be gathered from all nations will be greater than anyone can count. Finally, the vast and unthinkable numbers that were promised to Abraham—more than the stars of the sky, more than the grains of sand on the seashore—will materialize to enjoy the everlasting glory of this heavenly New Jerusalem.

Until that final glory arrives, however, tribulation and upheaval must occur while God works to set things right that had gone wrong. He will spread the Church to the four winds, that is, in every direction on earth, and together they will be known as "daughter of Zion." Masters and slaves will have their roles reversed, because the Lord will protect His own people just as carefully as someone protects his own eye from injury. The "apple" of the eye is the pupil, which was said to be especially delicate, vulnerable, and sensitive. The nations that once were plunderers will themselves be plundered in this divine act of judgment.

All of this is to be inaugurated on the day when the Lord Himself will come to dwell in the midst of men. When Jesus Christ, our Immanuel, came to this earth to be with us, then began the salvation for which the daughter of Zion would sing and rejoice. In this time of the New Testament Church, people from many nations will join themselves to the Lord in faith, for the spread of God's Word will encompass the earth. All of this will then come to its final fulfillment and consummation when our Lord Christ returns on the Last Day. In light of this mighty deed for which the Lord has roused Himself for action, the appropriate response of worship is (v. 13) "Be silent, all flesh, before the Lord."

4 Joshua Restored (Zechariah 3)

Perhaps the most memorable dreams are those that include people you know. That one memorable night, Zechariah was granted the rare occasion to see someone he knew personally, not in a dream, but in a divinely-inspired, vivid reality. God revealed to him a relative and fellow priest, Joshua—who was not only a priest, but he was also the high priest and representative for all the other priests as well as for all of Israel.

Joshua was seen standing before God (that is, the Angel of the Lord) dressed in filthy garments, and therefore unfit for his assigned service as high priest before the Lord. Because of this visual depiction of sin, Joshua was worthy of nothing but dismissal from the holy throne room. This was true not only for him personally, as it would be for any sinful human being, but also and especially because he was held accountable for the sin of the people whom he represented. Isaiah had lamented, (6:5) "Woe is me! For I am lost; for I am a man of unclean lips, and I dwell in the midst of a people of unclean lips." A similar twofold exposure of iniquity renders the high priest utterly speechless—he was sinful and he was representing sinful people.

But someone was talking! Standing there at Joshua's right hand—the position that normally connotes dependable help—was the accuser himself, Satan. Far from helping him, the father of lies was on this particular occasion prepared to tell God the truth about Judah's spiritual leader. His aim as an accuser is to misapply the wrath of the Lord against sinful man. This would crush believers into despair and convince them of his favorite falsehood: that the promises of God's love and forgiveness are somehow null and void.

Yet the old evil foe cannot prevail. Satan's going down. "One little word can fell him," as the hymn says. And that simple pronouncement is (v. 2) "The Lord rebuke you!" Yes, the human priest of God, along with the people he served, was destined for eternal fire, at least according to what he deserved. But because of our Lord's merciful redemption of sinful man paid for by the blood of Christ on a single day—Good Friday—Joshua and all believers were plucked like a smoldering brand from the fire. Satan will not take us down with him! He is forever rebuked, thanks to the death of Jesus.

Here we have in the middle of this string of visions the central jewel of biblical doctrine: the free and complete forgiveness of sins by God's grace, received through faith alone. The soiled and tattered garments were removed, and the pure vestments of righteousness were put on instead. Everything that Zechariah had seen so far had led up to this climactic scene; everything yet to come during this night of revelation would build from its foundational truth. The prophet himself could not stand by silently—he cried out with excitement, "Don't forget the clean turban!" And the angelic attendants got to work on Joshua's pure wardrobe while the Angel of the Lord looked on. Now that the high priest is properly vested, God's Son renews the ordination vow. The rights and privileges of office are guaranteed to Joshua, including the right of access into the Lord's own gracious throne room; but together with this came the solemn charge to remain faithful.

Finally, there was the stone that was placed in front of Joshua. What could this symbolic image be? As it reads, the Hebrew could go either way: does the stone itself have seven eyes, which may lead the interpreter to the alternate translation of "facets"; or is it instead *watched* by seven eyes, referring to God's perfect care and keeping over the Church, His precious, engraved possession? We will need further clues from Scripture to help us with this mystery. In the meantime, along with Zechariah, we may rejoice in the opportunity we've been given to invite our neighbors to enjoy with us the blessings of salvation.

5 The Day of Small Things (Zechariah 4)

As his unforgettable night of eight visions continues, Zechariah is jostled awake. However, the way this is recorded suggests that he was not sleeping in the normal sense of the word. The sensation he felt was (v. 1) "like a man who is awakened out of his sleep," a jolt that courses through your body like a lightning bolt just as you are drifting off, and for a while at least, the tired feeling subsides and you gain alertness.

Anyway, that sudden feeling of "I'm awake!" was what Zechariah experienced, and it makes little difference whether he was actually sleeping or was suddenly elevated to an even higher awareness of the spiritual visions that were to come. Similar to the other visions, there was an angel by his side, ready to dialogue with the prophet and explain what he had seen. He seemed persistent in an effort to make Zechariah come up with the explanation himself, and if he came up short, then the angel interpreter would help him out. Scripture deals with lofty truths, to be sure, but God's intent with all of His Word—even the apocalyptic visions—is to provide clarity for the believer, ensuring salvation's certainty. The Holy Bible is God's Book, written by the inspiration of the Holy Spirit Himself, but it is also meant for mankind so that we will not be befuddled or frightened of the Creator's wrath, but instead encounter Christ and see the full extent of His love for us sinners.

Priests had countless chores when it came to Old Testament worship. Many of them had to deal with the lamps for worship. It was a constant task just to keep the lamps burning. Put out the dim light, trim the wick, grab the container of olive oil, fill the reservoir, and relight from another lamp or flame.

But what did Zechariah see? A perpetual oil lamp! No refilling required! A magnificent contraption that is full of symbolism. It is depicted as a large golden bowl of oil that feeds seven lamps with seven lips, or channels, through which the oil fuels each flame. And to replenish the lampstand, there are two olive trees on either side, having the mysterious capability to juice their own endless supply of olives and then send the precious liquid gold down two pipes to feed the seven flames. Human ingenuity can only dream of such convenience! But God says, (v. 6) "Not by might, nor by power, but by My Spirit." What man says is impossible, the Lord perfectly accomplishes! Seven is God's perfect number, and the oil and flame refer to the Holy Spirit's activity in the Church. Two anointed leaders were standing ready to serve: in Zechariah's time, they were Joshua and Zerubbabel. These two anointed leaders point forward to our Lord Christ, who is for us both High Priest and King.

Zechariah's contemporaries were weary returning exiles. Not much had yet happened in their favor. But there was something comforting for them, something they would readily understand that would make them rejoice. God promised His people that the leader who laid the foundation of the rebuilt temple would also lay the final stone on top. And with the plumb line in Zerubbabel's hand, making sure everything that is dedicated to God was straight and sturdy, the people would shout, "Grace! Grace to it!" For all buildings, from that time all the way to our own, if they are dedicated to God's Word and distributing the gifts of forgiveness, are places full of grace, of which there will be a perpetual supply.

Conclusion

As we have read so far, Zechariah issued a general call for repentance and reported five of his night visions. Jerusalem and a renewed temple are a key focus of his messages, but there is something more to what the Lord was revealing to His prophet. The Angel of the Lord, a magnificent person in Zechariah's visions, will return in the fullness of time, on the true day of small things, wrapped in human flesh and swaddling cloths to be laid in a manger. At this, all the Church rejoices!

Concluding Activities

Conclude the session with an appropriate prayer and distribute the study leaflet for week 5.

The Coming of the Branch
Zechariah 5–8

Preparing for the Session

Central Focus

Zechariah continues to relay messages of God's judgment against the faithless and a renewal of prosperity for His believing people. Strange night visions give way to the Lord's clear and plain assurances of His presence and a new beginning, claiming Jerusalem and the temple as the focal point for long-awaited peace. God's people are reminded that they are a light to all nations, as the Savior's coming approaches.

Objectives

That participants, led by the Holy Spirit working through God's Word, will

1. take note of a significant shift in the Lord's method of revelation to Zechariah;
2. assimilate Zechariah's predictions of good news with the Gospel of Jesus Christ; and
3. gain motivation for the Church's mission today.

Note for the small-group leaders: Lesson notes and other materials you will need begin on page 71.

For the Lecture Leader

Session Plan

Worship

Begin the session with the hymn printed in the study leaflet. Accompaniments are available in denominational hymnals, such as *Lutheran Service Book* or *Lutheran Worship* (refer to hymnal index). (Note: Concordia Publishing House has available *The Concordia Organist*. All the initial worship hymns in the LifeLight courses are included in this resource. It's especially helpful for mission congregations and small parishes. See the list of study resources on p. 7.) Follow with this prayer:

Prayer

Lord God, heavenly Father, in these latter days, we beseech You to build Your Church and grant us strength to face the challenges of our society around us. Lead us to be merciful, just as Your Son, Jesus, during the ministry of His flesh, was merciful to all who sought Him in faith. Open our ears to hear Your precious Word that sustains Your people from day to day. And when the final day comes, the day when our Savior will return in glory, graciously receive us into the kingdom of glory that He has prepared for us through His sacrificial blood. In His name we pray. Amen.

Lecture Presentation

1 The Scroll and the Woman (Zechariah 5)

Zechariah's memorable night continued with more visions, and the next ones he saw became even more bizarre than the previous one. The messages behind the visions had also changed from comforting signs of grace and a hopeful future to warnings of divine judgment against evildoers.

Finally, things had been looking better for Zion as the habitation of the Lord. Zerubbabel would oversee the completion of the temple in Jerusalem. Joshua would be clothed in purified garments so that he could once again distribute forgiveness. These two anointed leaders, like fruitful olive branches, would never lack oil in their lamps as they stood ready to serve the Lord of the whole earth.

Suddenly, a foreboding vision interrupted all this good news that Zechariah has witnessed up to this point. He had returned to the subject of the original call to repentance that we read about in the very beginning of the book. There was a reason God's people needed to turn from their evil ways and refuse the temptation to act as their fathers did before the exile. He would still hold them accountable and would by no means clear the guilty people who remained in their sinful, unbelieving way of life. The Lord would come through on His promises to deliver Israel and make them prosper again in their own land, but He would also act with swift and decisive judgment on all who rejected His grace.

For Zechariah, that curse of judgment appeared in the form of a flying scroll. As it soared through the air, the prophet saw it unrolling over the land. It seemed like the words written on the scroll were a kind of vulture or eagle, spreading out wings and circling about the land, ready to pounce on unsuspecting prey. Both sides of this papyrus roll were filled with God's writing, and the angel guide explained to Zechariah just who would be the target of its deathly strike. Two types of hardened sinners were singled out: those who steal and those who swear falsely by the name of the Lord. It's not as though these sins were the only ones that would be punished, while others would be tolerated. Rather, these are simply the two examples of sins that were committed both against God and man. The judgment of God, as pictured by the scroll, would clean these evildoers out of the land and utterly consume their houses, destroying both wood and stone without distinction.

Where would these evildoers go? That was answered by the following vision—yet another strange sight. Think of a hot-air balloon taking off, but there's no balloon! There was just a woman riding in a floating basket. In Hebrew, this basket is called an *ephah* after the unit of measurement it could hold in the everyday world. In the world of Zechariah's visions, however, this basket was removing the wickedness from the land of God's chosen people. Zechariah's angel companion shoved the female personification of iniquity under a lead weight to ensure that it did not escape and return to destroy the Promised Land.

Two other women, flying with the wings of a soaring stork, were seen taking the basket to the land of Shinar, the ancient plain where the tower of Babel had been built and then abandoned. It signified for the Israelites the home base of all people who were locked in rebellion against God. Even though Shinar was in the vicinity where the exiles used to live in Babylon, this vision was not signifying that a new exile was being threatened. Instead, it was meant to ensure that God's abundant grace would not be used as a crutch for sin in this new era that had begun for His chosen people.

2 The Branch Builds the Temple (Zechariah 6)

Zechariah's night of visions began with colorful horses sent out to patrol the earth. It would come to a conclusion with chariots drawn by teams of horses of slightly different colors. These horses would be sent with a mission that would set at rest the Spirit of the Lord as He was engaged in judgment. The prophet witnessed these four chariots bursting forth from between two bronze mountains as though they were the starting gates of a race. Bronze was the strongest metal available; two mountains of bronze would have been absolutely immovable and indestructible. The horses were rippling with strength and eagerness to run, meaning God's will would be accomplished swiftly and with decisive power, both for judgment and for vindication of a lowly, yet still chosen people. The black horses, which had not appeared in the first vision, reflect a divine mission of judgment and devastation. They were sent to the north, referring to Babylonia and Assyria, because those nations had approached and attacked the Holy Land from that direction. The Spirit of the Lord had been set at rest in the north because those two nations, which had been involved in God's punishment of Israel and Judah, had finally themselves been conquered. Zechariah was aware that King Darius of Persia had been in power for two years by this time, so those old enemies of the Lord's people would never again raise their hands against them. They, too, might rest in the peace that God Himself had restored for them in their land.

Suddenly, the visions broke off for Zechariah, and he received a spoken word from the Lord. The prophet was instructed to assemble a small group of recently returned exiles, and they would help him fashion a crown made from their offerings of silver and gold. It would seem that this crown was to be composed of several circlets made from the two precious metals and woven or fused together—the image might make you think of the hymn "Crown Him with Many Crowns." Yet the recipient of this crown would have caused Zechariah and his companions to pause at least a moment with bewilderment. Why would Joshua get the crown? The high priest was fully vested with his priestly clothing, including a turban for his head; nevertheless, he was being treated like a king in this unique ceremony.

What reason would the Lord give for crowning the high priest? It would be to set up the next magnificent prophetic Word that He would plant on the lips of Zechariah—yet another proclamation of Jesus Christ Himself. Christ is the true Royal Priest, a Savior who fulfills both roles of King and Priest simultaneously. All who believe in Him and are baptized in the era of the New Testament will also enter the royal priesthood in His name. Not only Joshua by himself, but Joshua and Zerubbabel together prefigure Jesus as both Priest and King. The crown will stay at the newly finished temple as a testimony to the one God-man who would be truly worthy to wear it.

In this Word of the Lord, the Messiah is revealed by the name of the Branch (v. 12), a name that was well-attested in Scripture before the exile, especially by Isaiah and Jeremiah. The Branch was briefly mentioned during the vision of Joshua (3:8), but here the Lord granted a full disclosure of what this title means and what the Messiah would be sent to do. The idea behind the name is a shoot or stalk that springs up from the ground once a large tree is cut down (see Isaiah 11:1). The Virgin-born Savior would spring up metaphorically from the very ground of the Promised Land, branching out all over the earth through the preaching of His Word. He would perfectly and completely build the spiritual temple of the Lord. The Church will continue to be built thanks to the "living stones" from all nations far off (2 Peter 2:5)—all who faithfully trust in our Lord's all-sufficient Word.

3 Fasting without Faith (Zechariah 7)

Nearly two years had passed for Zechariah since his night of eight visions. Bolstered by Zechariah's encouraging, inspired words, the people were hard at work rebuilding the temple. All in Jerusalem and in the surrounding lands were strengthened in hope as they waited with eager expectation for the coming of their Savior. Yet while their attention was being turned to a positive future and a renewed worship of God, the memories of the past needed sufficient resolution in the minds of many of these humbled believers.

When a family, a community, or a nation commemorates a tragedy, how long is long enough to remember? Will anniversaries of D-day, Pearl Harbor, or even September 11 eventually fade in the mind of our culture? Or will these bloody tragedies of years past be transformed into an even greater remembrance that will bring strength and peace to all who continue to call them to mind? The inhabitants of the city of Bethel had a question for the Lord's priests concerning a commemorative fast that recalled the fall of Jerusalem at the hands of the Babylonians. For nearly seventy years, the people had been observing this commemoration, and soon the temple rebuilding project would be complete. Would the cause of this fast then be rendered obsolete, relegated to the dusty volumes of ancient history? Perhaps they were looking for God's directions on whether it was time for His people to move on with their lives.

Even though the emissaries from Bethel had asked their question to the priests, the Lord wanted Zechariah to answer in His stead to everyone, whether priest or layperson. He reminded them of the "former prophets," that is, the men speaking for God before the time of the Babylonian exile. Back in days of prosperity, when the cities weren't yet the ghost towns they had become, prophets had preached and proclaimed until they were blue in the face, yet no one at the time wanted to hear. When their Israelite descendants returned from the land of exile and reclaimed their inherited homeland, they continued to fast and recall the horrible events of the past. But they were forgetting why the devastation and exile happened in the first place. As Zechariah pointed out, they were marking this observance not for the Lord but for themselves.

What is fasting? It is a bodily exercise, a self-discipline that, if one so chooses, ought to be occasioned by faith. It can be used to keep our attention fixed on Christ, the Author of our faith, but fasting by itself is not faith. The prophet answered the people of Bethel's question on fasting by saying, in effect, "Before you start worrying about the details of your piety, you need to remember to hold firmly to your faith!" Yet getting the people to repent was like trying to saddle up a bucking bronco. They made their hearts "diamond-hard," and their ears were swollen shut. Their name of their city, Bethel, meant "house of God," but God's own Law revealed that faith was lacking within its walls. They could try to deceive others by showing how well they could deprive themselves of food, but in reality they were depriving their neighbors of justice, mercy, and love as the proper fruits of their faith.

The point of Zechariah's sermon to the men of Bethel was not to say whether it was right or wrong to commemorate an event in history. Rather, he wanted them to repent and to resist repeating the pattern of life that seventy years ago led to the exile. Without forgiveness and faith, their fasting would be a worthless sham. One could properly observe any day as an act of faith in the Lord, so long as forgiveness first made the heart right with Him. Doing it to earn God's favor for yourself would actually *separate* you from Him. When a certain scribe answered Jesus saying that genuine love toward God and neighbor is greater than any purely outward show of worship, the Savior commended him, (Mark 12:34) "You are not far from the kingdom of God."

4 The Lord Will Sow Peace (Zechariah 8:1–13)

On the first occasion when the Lord uttered ten holy "words," or sayings, to the children of men, the scene was high on Mount Sinai. Moses carried those words down the mountain on two tablets of stone. Several centuries later, Zechariah recorded in this chapter a new set of ten words of the Lord, each of them introduced by the repeated phrase "Thus says the LORD of hosts." Apparently following the example of Moses himself, the later prophet sounds rather emphatic about his role as spokesman for God.

Right from the start, Zechariah's list bears a resemblance to the Ten Commandments, in which the Lord cited His unique quality of "jealousy." When the First Commandment, "You shall have no other gods before Me," was originally decreed on the holy mountain, it was prefaced with the recollection of the Lord's great act of rescue: (Exodus 20:2) "I am the LORD your God, who brought you out of the land of Egypt." Then immediately after this fountainhead commandment comes what is called "The Close of the Commandments." It reads, (Exodus 20:5–6) "For I the LORD your God am a jealous God, visiting the iniquity of the fathers on the children to the third and fourth generation of those who hate Me, but showing steadfast love to thousands of those who love Me and keep My commandments."

God's jealousy is tied up in His fervent desire for us to live according to His will, yet it is also combined with His anger because we have utterly disobeyed Him through our sins. You and I may become jealous when we feel that we have been betrayed or treated unfairly at the hands of another. Our heavenly Father, however, is the only one who has the pure, legitimate claim to jealousy because He is the ultimate target of our sin (Psalm 51:4). No matter what commandments we have broken, no matter how great or trivial, we have most certainly broken faith with our Creator, who has every right to exclude us from His presence forever.

This time, the Lord's jealousy turns out to be good news for Israel, emphasizing the part about His steadfast love for the thousands. Even though Jerusalem and its surrounding lands were at this point still sparsely populated with returning pilgrims, we see here recorded the promise that God Himself would dwell in the midst of His replanted remnant. Because of the Lord's presence alone, Jerusalem shall be known as the faithful city, the holy mountain. And in the fullness of time, when the Lord's presence eventually would come in the flesh of Jesus, the crucified and risen Messiah, the New Jerusalem of the Christian Church would have superseded the tired, old, Middle East city that was encouraged by centuries of prophets to wait for His coming.

The returning exiles couldn't wait for better times to come to their beloved former capital. They yearned for both young and old to be numerous in Jerusalem's streets. They needed many strong hands to accompany them in building, planting, reaping, and defending. Prophets were there when the new temple's foundation was laid, and they still spoke as the people cried out for encouragement. The question was would they continue to hear God's Word and believe? Or would this small remnant despair of the Lord's promise to save? Would they remain fearful of the many nations who had cursed their very existence? Let the anxieties be gone with one more divine word: "Fear not." Not only would the Lord again bless His people, but He would also guarantee to them that they themselves would be a blessing to others, a repetition of His original promise to Abraham in Genesis 12.

5 How to Retain the Blessing (Zechariah 8:14–23)

The ten words from the Lord of hosts continue as we proceed through chapter 8. The beautiful, heavenly command of comfort, "Fear not," was repeated. When God threatened disaster, He delivered on His threat because the faithless forefathers had stirred up God's wrath. But wrath is not in the Lord's true nature, or as it can be said, wrath is part of God's "alien work." He must respond in wrath and anger against sin, which He did not create and which cannot exist in His holy presence. God's "proper work" is to love and create good things, which He does after tearing down the bad. Zechariah was inspired to assure his congregation, "You were aware that when God had it in mind to punish the previous generations, He did not change His mind and hold back His anger from them. Well, now He has bound Himself not to destroy you, but to love you and bring days of good to you and all believers. You can count on that promise coming true, even more so because it is His true nature to bring you blessing."

What could the people do to ensure that this blessing would stay with them for generations? That should have been the number one thought in the minds of former exiles as they were rebuilding the demolished temple stone by stone—what will keep disaster like this from afflicting us again? Here Zechariah referred them back to the Ten Commandments. Love your neighbor as God has loved you and saved you. Speak the truth to one another, and do not make evil, self-serving plans in your hearts. If you rest in the Lord's forgiveness and then turn back and pursue the very actions He hates, you show your disdain of the things that make for peace.

This is not to say that salvation by grace is thrust aside and now you are on your own to make it the rest of the way by your works. Instead, the point is to allow the new creation that is planted in your heart to take root and grow into a life of good works that spreads the free grace of God to those around you like ever-expanding tree of life. Thanks to the Holy Spirit, the believer is blessed and then becomes a blessing to others.

In the previous chapter, Zechariah answered a question about fasting that was posed to the priests on behalf of the people of Bethel. Their ritual remembrance of the Babylonian invasion and captivity included times of fasting in addition to those occasions God had originally commanded. Here in chapter 8, we discover that there had been a string of four observances connected with events from those dark days, each marked with a fast: the fourth, fifth, seventh, and tenth months. These somber observances marked by the lack of eating would, under the Lord's blessing, be festivals of joy and gladness—not to mention feasting! Pilgrims will resume going to the presence of the Lord, and people will encourage one another along the way: "Come along with me! I'm going myself!" When you seek the favor of the merciful God of all Israel, unbelievers observing you will actually seek you out! Remain faithful to Him, and they'll grab you by the robe of Christ's righteousness, saying, "Let us go with you, for we have heard that God is with you." When God makes His grace evident in your life, you won't be able to keep away the ones who are truly searching for the blessing you have. It is the best evangelism tool yet!

Conclusion

Zechariah takes an intermission at this point in the book, but there is more to come in this messianic concert. Beginning with chapter 9, the writing style changes somewhat, leading some to wonder whether another author is taking over the baton. Yet the same basic themes of judgment, restoration, and future prosperity will continue, building in a crescendo toward events and images that Jesus Himself would employ during His featured solo performance.

Concluding Activities

Conclude the session with an appropriate prayer and distribute the study leaflet for week 6.

The Shepherd Saves the Sheep

Zechariah 9–11

Preparing for the Session

Central Focus

Zechariah's earlier visions and prophecies have been building up to a grand revealing of the Messiah, the coming Savior. He foretells destruction for God's enemies, the triumphant King riding on a donkey, the Messiah's saving victory for the faithful people, and doom for the people who in unbelief sold Him off, as Judas would do. Although disaster and judgment run rampant in this section, the focus still remains positive for believers.

Objectives

That participants, led by the Holy Spirit working through God's Word, will

1. notice the familiar messianic passages and see them in their original context;
2. verify the true Old Testament hope in Jesus' person and work; and
3. reject the illegitimate expectations of a shallow "gospel" of worldly prosperity.

Note for the small-group leaders: Lesson notes and other materials you will need begin on page 74.

For the Lecture Leader

Session Plan

Worship

Begin the session with the hymn printed in the study leaflet. Accompaniments are available in denominational hymnals, such as *Lutheran Service Book* or *Lutheran Worship* (refer to hymnal index). (Note: Concordia Publishing House has available *The Concordia Organist*. All the initial worship hymns in the LifeLight courses are included in this resource. It's especially helpful for mission congregations and small parishes. See the list of study resources on p. 7.) Follow with this prayer:

Prayer

We rejoice, O Lord Jesus, our King, in Your lowly coming among us, humbly wrapped first in flesh and blood and now given to us in Word, water, bread, and wine. We admit, as a struggling, tempted, stubborn, and battered daughter of Zion, that we have done what is worthy of nothing but punishment now and forever. But we thank You for Your full and ultimate salvation, which You won for us on the cross and proclaimed through the empty tomb, and for Your words of peace. Forgive us our sins and grant us new hearts to shout and sing aloud for joy so that all the world may know of the eternal life that You won for our sake and for the rescue of all people. Grant this for the sake of Your holy name. Amen.

Lecture Presentation

1 Enemies Cut Down (Zechariah 9:1–8)

The seminary graduate is brimming with excitement on his ordination day. He gets up from his special chair of honor in front of the whole congregation and is flanked on both sides by veteran pastors. Stepping closer to the altar, the candidate looks forward in expectation to the officiant standing in front of him. The ceremony goes by in a blur; the soon-to-be pastor tries to grasp all those holy words of Scripture that are whizzing by, words that testify to God's establishment of the Office of the Holy Ministry. Then, his nerves electrify as hands are laid on him, though not in any magical or mysterious sense. These hands declare that the words being spoken are meant for *you*! Finally, the well-known symbol of the pastoral office—the strip of fine cloth known as the stole—is draped over his shoulders. This simple ritual in the ceremony testifies to the duties and responsibilities he has assumed. From this day onward, a burden to preach the Gospel, in season and out of season, rests on the man whom the Lord of the Church has called. Every time this new pastor wears the stole, he will be reminded of the yoke of Christ and his own solemn promise to bear up that load with the help and comfort of the Holy Spirit.

He may never have worn a stole, but all the same, the prophet Zechariah received his own burden from the

Lord. Usually a word of prophecy in the Old Testament is called a "burden" when it includes severe judgment for the intended hearers. Of course, it would be a difficult task to be the bearer of bad news. But Zechariah had a holy calling; he would answer not to flesh and blood but to the lofty judgment throne of God Almighty. The burden is the same whether you're talking about an Old Testament prophet or a New Testament servant of the Word.

There was one thing going for him, though. Zechariah's burden of negative prophecy, at least at this point, was directed against foreign nations. He was not sent this time to chastise his own people. The burden of the Word of the Lord instead rested on lands and cities that lay to the north of Israel. Hadrach, Damascus, Hamath, Tyre, and Sidon are to be warned that their days are numbered. The Phoenician colonial city of Tyre, a fortress situated on a rocky island off the Mediterranean coast, was considered impenetrable. Gold was piled up in heaps as though it were trash. Silver accumulated like dust. The place was wealthy and well-protected. But that would not deter the Lord's swift stroke of justice.

Other nations would do well to take note of this burden of prophecy recorded by Zechariah. Down the coastline from Tyre sat the prominent cities of the Philistines, those ever-present enemies of Israel who dominated the seas. God would open their eyes so that they would take notice when He struck those northern strongholds. Their national pride would then melt away in fear. God had a plan for His chosen people that would not waver, and these enemies would not be permitted to last much longer. Here we see that Zechariah dons the stole of his prophetic burden to clear away the obstacles, so that his magnificent sermon of Gospel comfort can have free course. He may have been just as excited as a new pastor on his ordination day!

2 Rejoice Greatly! (Zechariah 9:9–13)

When the Lord fulfills His promises, that is truly a cause for His chosen people to rejoice! Zechariah let loose the brilliant words of encouragement that the Holy Spirit placed on his lips. The Messiah Himself is prophesied parading into the Holy City in all His Palm Sunday glory. You almost get the impression that the prophet could see the entire opening scene of Holy Week, five hundred years into the future. People were strewing their garments along the road and waving palm branches in the afternoon sun as the Lord and His humble donkey passed into the shadow made by Jerusalem's wall. Shouts of hosanna drown out every other noise that was coming from the assembled crowd. The rejoicing was truly great.

In his proclamation, however, Zechariah used a name that would certainly capture attention from his hearers, and most certainly it was not flattering. "Daughter of Zion" and "daughter of Jerusalem" sounded like slaps in the face. These terms did not mean a single person; rather, they referred to all the inhabitants of this important city, taken together as though they were one collective "daughter." Hearing "daughter of Zion" would have reminded them of the past, of the exile in particular. It recalled what Jeremiah wrote as he looked out on the scorched and wasted leftovers of Jerusalem, (Lamentations 2:1) "How the Lord in His anger has set the daughter of Zion under a cloud!" When the people of Jerusalem were called "daughter of Zion," they were reminded of the sting of their sins against God and His utter punishment from which they were just beginning to recover. Why bring up that sore subject now?

It seems like the daughter of Zion was always in trouble. She was the sheep that loved to stray, looking for better pasture in the fields of a master besides her God. Seventy years might have gone by since that utter destruction, but the same rebellious sinful nature that had brought on the exile was still inside these hearers, the daughter of Jerusalem. They continued to feel the nagging doubts that were afflicting them. Uncertainty about the future still threatened to weaken their resolve. When the residents of Jerusalem were called "daughter of Zion," it meant they had to face the hard truth that by themselves they were helpless—they needed a Savior.

These words were a perfect message of Gospel peace for people about to finish the once-destroyed temple, as they are also fitting for us today. The Church is full of doubting, frightened, anxious sinners like the ones we see every day in the mirror, so the terms "daughter of Zion" and "daughter of Jerusalem" work as though Zechariah were speaking to us today, which he is! Our reason to rejoice greatly and shout aloud in praise is precisely because our King Jesus has come to us just as God's Word promised He would. He is not a thought or an idea that we call up from inside our own hearts. He is a Savior who invaded our sinful earth to speak the perfect peace of His death and resurrection to all nations. His rule over His redeemed Church shall be from sea to sea.

When Christ fulfilled Zechariah's prophecy on the first Palm Sunday, He achieved salvation for us no less than

He did for the people who had seen Him with their own eyes. Jesus may not be riding on a lowly donkey for us today, but He is hidden in the lowly forms we do witness among us: words of preaching, water of Baptism, bread and wine of the Lord's Supper. This is the procession that makes us rejoice, because we don't come to church merely to remind ourselves of the idea of a past Jesus—we come to meet our present Savior, who is pleased to dwell among us still! Thanks to His true blood of the eternal covenant, we the prisoners have been set free.

3 God's Trumpet (Zechariah 9:14–17)

The King is not coming just to parade around town on a donkey. Instead, the Lord of hosts is coming to do battle! Armed with the sword of His almighty Word, God's people themselves are His weapons against unbelief and Satan's arsenal that is engaged against them. The sound of the trumpet will signal that the final, decisive blow is imminent. He will attack like a whirlwind from the south, that is, a thunderstorm that leads with a wilting blast of hot air. Those enemies will have no defense against His unparalleled strength.

The sounding of the trumpet (v. 14) is at once a military and liturgical activity. Old Testament priest and military commander alike placed their lips to the narrow end of a ram's horn, which in Hebrew is called the *shofar*. Well-known is the battle of Jericho, fought exclusively with the priests sounding trumpets and the army marching laps around the city wall for seven days. The trumpet always signaled the commencement of divine activity. It was especially prominent in the Day of Atonement ceremony in the seventh month of the Hebrew calendar—it heralded the authorization for the high priest to enter the Most Holy Place and offer the sacrifice of atonement, that is, the payment for sin, for the whole people. In apocalyptic visions, the liturgical trumpet blast meant that evil forces were about to be defeated and destroyed.

A battle would not be complete without lots of bloodshed! Enemies of God will be so thoroughly massacred that their blood will pour out like endless bowls of wine, making the soldiers of the Lord shout like drunks! Without condoning the debauchery of drunkenness (Ephesians 5:18), the image was meant to emphasize the decisive blow that would be inflicted against the adversary. Bowls of blood, reminiscent of the temple sacrifices in which the drained blood of animals was thrown on the corners of the altar, likewise indicate an outcome of utter victory for those who are on the Lord's side.

After the time of war comes the messianic peace. This is introduced with the important phrase "on that day" (v. 16). Once the enemies are completely defeated, the Lord's people may enjoy the benefits of their salvation. As the hymn sings, "This day the din of battle, The next the victor's song" (*LSB* 660:4). Though it may seem endless, the fighting will not endure forever. Before, the people of God were His weapons; now, after the conflict is over, they are called His flock. Zechariah returned to this important spiritual image in a following section when He described their Shepherd in greater detail.

In verse 16, the prophet hands to his hearers the promise that the Lord greatly values His chosen nation. When victory is finally achieved, the people themselves shine in their allotted land like jewels sparkling in the crown of the Christ-King. Each believer is bought with the precious blood of the cross of Jesus. Therefore, each believer himself is precious in the sight of the heavenly Father. How great is His goodness! How great is His beauty! In verse 17, the glory of God's new creation is described in terms of abundant grain and new wine, the two main food staples of vigorous youth. In the life of the world to come, the signs of feeble old age will be a distant memory.

4 Strong in the Lord (Zechariah 10)

Brighter days were on the horizon for the chosen people of God as they came closer to the arrival of the Messiah, the King who would come mounted on a donkey. Zechariah described this salvation using various images of prosperity, abundance, and success in battle. He was urging the people to cash in their chips! Claim the benefits of being a privileged, chosen nation. Call on the Lord, because He desires to give good gifts. Don't let a good thing go to waste—believe that God will provide and then receive it: (Psalm 81:10) "Open your mouth wide," says the Lord, "and I will fill it." He is going to make His people strong as they walk in His name.

The prophet launched right into some examples of this rich generosity that the Lord can't wait to dole out. Is it rain that you need? Ask for it! Don't worry that it is getting late in the season. That would betray a lack of confident faith. If you get just the right amount of rain in the spring, in addition to what you already received in the temperate Mediterranean winter months, then your harvest will be extra-plentiful. There's nothing wrong with a bumper crop of blessings! After all, who makes the storm clouds, anyway? The Lord will give the showers of rain that you need. Ask, and He will provide.

But, you may ask, isn't that what those shallow preachers of prosperity constantly tell us today? You can just hear their sales pitch: "Yes, sir! You will be healthy, wealthy, and wise if you believe hard enough that God will make you successful." What is missing in this approach to prayer, however, is Jesus as the object of faith; He is prayer's perfect answer. Your heavenly Father is not going to give blessings because you said the right words or did something worthy of a reward. If you were to believe that, then you would actually be denying Christ and behaving like a pagan! Plus, there is the reminder that Paul gave about blessings for the present age: (1 Corinthians 15:19) "If in Christ we have hope in this life only, we are of all people most to be pitied." To be sure, we receive all things from the Father only because of Christ, yet Jesus died and rose from the dead not because we needed good things in this life, but because we were separated from our Creator and needed a Savior to bring us the greatest blessing: eternal life. (Matthew 6:33) "Seek first the kingdom of God and His righteousness, and all these things will be added to you." When the priorities of faith are correct, we are promised both heavenly and temporal blessings in their proper proportion.

So what is Zechariah's point in urging the people to pray for rain, to ditch the false gods, to gain confidence in military strength over their foes? He wanted them to remain assured that the Lord would provide all that they needed. He was eager to cultivate their faith and make it strong, as it was for Israel back in the days of King David. He desired to reveal the abundant mercy of God to forgive sins and restore peace with Him and with one another. Even the centuries-old split of Northern Kingdom and Southern Kingdom was not too great an obstacle for the Lord to reconcile the two and make a strong, faithful, and united people out of their modest numbers. With the Messiah coming, all of this was possible, and He would establish the Christian Church as His flock, which will never pass away, no matter what battles that flock may face.

5 Thirty Pieces of Silver (Zechariah 11)

What happened, Zechariah? You had just predicted in chapter 10 a time of strength and plenty, and all because of the coming of the Messiah, right? So why, in chapter 11, are we back on the subject of punishment, even slaughter? Like a splash of cold water in the face, there is a surprising, sudden announcement of destruction headed for the northern reaches of the Holy Land: the forests of Lebanon in the northwest, the oaks of Bashan to the northeast, and the thicket of vegetation around the headwaters of the Jordan River—all ruined! Something very wrong is about to take place as the Christ establishes His everlasting kingdom.

What Zechariah was, in fact, granted to see in his day was the future rejection of Jesus: (Psalm 118:22; Matthew 21:42) "the stone that the builders rejected." But instead of a vision, like in chapters 1–6, or a directly revealed utterance, as he received in chapters 7–10, the prophet was at this point called on to act out certain symbolic prophecies. He wasn't required to go to great extremes as Ezekiel had to do: lie on his side and eat whole grain cakes (Ezekiel 4:9–17). Unlike Hosea (1:2), he was *not* told to marry an unfaithful prostitute and explain her as a symbol of God's unfaithful nation. Instead, Zechariah in his particular "action prophecy" was told to play the role of Jesus. Zechariah was to act the part of the Good Shepherd who had come to His own people, yet God had doomed them to slaughter because they rejected their own Messiah. Yes, he was to predict the judgment and destruction of the Jewish nation that would eventually follow their denial and crucifixion of Jesus, as well as their persecution of His early followers. Claiming to uphold their religious integrity, they accused Jesus of blasphemy and turned Him over to the slaughterers. The leaders of Israel, the shepherds whom God placed over His people, were pitiless tyrants, so the Lord refused to show them any more pity.

Zechariah broke the two symbolic staffs that represented God's fulfillment of His promise, because the people would reject their own Savior. The unity and brotherhood they once enjoyed as fellow exiles joined together in a fresh start would also be broken. Then, in anticipation of what Judas would do five centuries later, the prophet took thirty pieces of silver from the dishonest sheep traders and threw them into the Lord's house. Jesus would have a price on His head, and thirty pieces of silver would be the wages due to the shepherd whose flock was doomed to destruction because of their rebellion. Just as Zechariah described in detail the joyous event of Palm Sunday, he was also inspired to predict our Lord's betrayal into the hands of sinners.

Finally, Zechariah was told to play another role. This time, he would act out what a foolish shepherd would do, who would not feed or care for the flock, but instead would devour and exploit them. Then, the Lord would have him pronounce His summary judgment: (v. 17) "Woe to my worthless shepherd, who deserts the flock!" The worthless shepherd's arm and eye—the parts of the shepherd's body most concerned about the welfare of the sheep—would be maimed and blinded, so that the unfaithful shepherd would no longer be a shepherd. The unfaithfulness of God's chosen servant leads many to eternal fire. Jesus similarly meant business when He threatened: (Matthew 18:6) "Whoever causes one of these little ones who believe in Me to sin, it would be better for him to have a great millstone fastened around his neck and to be drowned in the depth of the sea."

Conclusion

With Jesus now in full view within the prophetic tapestry of Zechariah, we have finally discovered the goal toward which all the previous visions and messages and calls for repentance were leading, one thread at a time. Having reached this climax, the Lord allows His prophet to develop in further detail how the Christ would accomplish His task of salvation. He also continues to call attention to the consequences that will plague those who reject His labors of love.

Concluding Activities

Conclude the session with an appropriate prayer and distribute the study leaflet for week 7.

All Nations Shall Worship Him

Zechariah 12–14

Preparing for the Session

Central Focus

Zechariah's final written prophecy stays focused on the Messiah, vividly portraying Good Friday events and proclaiming victory in His suffering and death on the cross. Zechariah ties these important events together with the inauguration of that favorite prophetic event known as the "Day of the Lord," the time at which full vindication for God's people will be revealed. With this promise as his closing word, his mission to encourage the weary remnant is complete.

Objectives

That participants, led by the Holy Spirit working through God's Word, will

1. apply the prophecies of the "Day of the Lord" to the time of the Christian Church;
2. praise God for the strong witness to Jesus Christ in the Old Testament; and
3. yearn for the spread of God's Word and complete salvation to all nations.

Note for the small-group leaders: Lesson notes and other materials you will need begin on page 78.

For the Lecture Leader

Session Plan

Worship

Begin the session with the hymn printed in the study leaflet. Accompaniments are available in denominational hymnals, such as *Lutheran Service Book* or *Lutheran Worship* (refer to hymnal index). (Note: Concordia Publishing House has available *The Concordia Organist.* All the initial worship hymns in the LifeLight courses are included in this resource. It's especially helpful for mission congregations and small parishes. See the list of study resources on p. 7.) Follow with this prayer:

Prayer

O Christ, our Good Shepherd, on the cross You were struck with suffering and death for the deliverance of Your precious sheep. You were pierced through with deadly wounds so that we might be healed from our sins. We pray that, as You promised salvation to Your people through the mouth of Zechariah long ago, You would in our day encourage us with that same Gospel Word of forgiveness and eternal life, until the final day when You return in glory and we are fully ransomed from the tribulations of this world. Hear us for the sake of Your holy name. Amen.

Lecture Presentation

1 A Heavy Stone (Zechariah 12:1–9)

One last time, Zechariah carried the burden of a prophetic utterance, this time not about foreign lands, but about Israel. For centuries, the name "Israel" referred only to the Northern Kingdom. These ten tribes broke off from Judah and Benjamin, but more important, their leaders broke the people off from the worship of the true God in Jerusalem. The Southern Kingdom, collectively named Judah, continued to be ruled by the house of David, but Israel was led astray by one evil king after another, until Assyria attacked them and ended their status as a nation. Judah held out on its own only a little while longer, but then they, too, fell when Babylon destroyed Jerusalem. So the split between North and South, Israel and Judah, seemed to be permanently etched in stone until Persia allowed people to return to the region. Then there arose the hope for a reunited Israel. They would not have their own king like Solomon or David ruling over them, but they would at least have Jerusalem and the temple as the focal point of their new life together as a nation. Zechariah was privileged to speak the Word of God that would encourage them to remain united and together prepare for the coming of the world's Savior.

First of all, Israel should be reminded that the God who brought them back to their land, who makes all these promises to them through the prophets—this God has been around the block before. He stretched out the very heavens at creation and set the earth on its foundations.

The Lord our God put our breath, our spirit, within us. This means He truly knows what's going on! He's in charge and is more than qualified to act in our best interest. The debate about evolution cannot be resolved as a simple interpretation of symbolic language. Our origins are not a trivial subject about which we can resign ourselves to understand in any number of ways. If we simply evolved in this universe by chance and do not have a Creator, then all the rest of the Christian faith is a man-made farce. It would follow that our unbelieving critics turn out to be correct after all, and we are imposing arbitrary views on others that nobody should be obligated to follow. Evolution demands there be no God, and where there is no God, then religion is a joke, and we are lost.

Based on the historical fact of our creation by the hands of our loving God, we then, as His Holy Church, can rest secure that He will protect us and grant us prosperity as He pleases. Even though enemies will line themselves up, intent on drinking down Jerusalem as though it were a cup of sweet wine, God Himself will make those attackers stagger with drunkenness so that they will not prevail over His Church. They will try to dislodge God's people, but Jerusalem shall be as a heavy stone that will hurt anyone who attempts to lift it out of its place. Such strength is not acquired by chance nor by personal effort—it comes from the Lord of hosts alone.

To highlight the Lord as the sole source of salvation, God reversed the expected order. Usually the fortress city of Jerusalem would be delivered first, and then gradually the wealth would spread to the outlying areas. Instead, so that the glory of one part of the Church would not surpass the other part, the tent-dwellers in the land of Judah will have first priority, bearing witness to the God whose (2 Corinthians 12:9) "power is made perfect in weakness." Indeed, the weak will be as strong as David, who prevailed over the giant Goliath with a sling and a stone. The house of David shall be like God, because little Bethlehem, the city of David, shall be the birthplace of the Son of God. He is the great Angel of the Lord who finally came among the people of earth to fulfill all the promises that God had made since creation.

2 Look on the One They Pierced (Zechariah 12:10–14)

A Good Friday service seems to attract worshipers in a unique way. Week after week, of course, the preaching of the Church is obligated to proclaim that Jesus Christ died for our sins. But when you get to the actual day that marks our Lord's crucifixion, it's almost like you're handed the opportunity to participate in the event yourself. The haunting spiritual sings, "Were you there when they crucified my Lord?" (*LSB* 456:1). No, to speak bluntly, you and I weren't there. But even if we had been there as part of the crowd, we would not have received the forgiveness won for us there. We receive the gifts of Good Friday as the Word is spoken to us, as the water is washed over us in Baptism, and when we eat and drink the body and blood given and shed for us.

That being said, we are still confronted with the event itself when we walk into church on Good Friday. We ought to be reminded that in our solemnities, we are not conducting a funeral for Christ. Instead, as the familiar readings and hymns spur our meditation and we follow our Savior on the way of sorrows to Calvary's hill, we pray that the Holy Spirit would breathe true repentance in our hearts. Only with genuine faith do we mourn our sins, the sins that caused such depths of suffering, and ponder the overflowing love spilled out with every drop of blood that flowed from the wounds of Christ crucified. Good Friday horrifies us, yet it also beautifully comforts us. That must be why we keep coming every year, looking forward to its unique tone and ceremony.

Zechariah looked forward to Good Friday with an eager heart too. As he was quoting God in this prophecy, a vivid scene from Golgotha emerged: (v. 10) "When they look on Me, on Him whom they have pierced, they shall mourn." Yes! God was pierced! And those who did it will realize their deed and mourn. Many commentators refuse to understand why God would speak of Himself as pierced; instead, they take the word to mean "insulted" or something like that. They tell themselves that God is spirit and so is incapable of suffering and death. How can He be killed? Only in one way—if He were to come to earth wrapped in human flesh and temporarily lay aside His almighty powers in utter humiliation for our sake, then Zechariah's prophecy would make perfect sense. Jesus Christ, the Son of God, did just that. His death was God's death, as Peter preached to the Jews in Jerusalem: (Acts 3:15) "You killed the Author of life, whom God raised from the dead." If the Author of life is not God, then we have problems! When the Roman soldier pierced the dead Son of God instead of breaking His legs (John 19:34–37), he fulfilled this prophecy of Zechariah.

Soon after Pentecost, the Spirit of grace was poured out on those who once were God's enemies and who, by their sins, had pierced Jesus. This holy conversion led sinners to plea for mercy, so that in mourning for their

Lord, with a heartfelt sorrow unmatched since before the exile, they would become the new house of David—the Holy Christian Church. This same outpouring of the Spirit occurs in all believers down to this very day who hear the Word of God, repent, and are baptized for the forgiveness of sins. Faith is planted in the heart, and the blessings of Good Friday lead us onward to the joy of Easter's resurrection!

3 Excising Idolatry (Zechariah 13:1–6)

When Jesus was pierced on the cross, His dead body became a fountain of blood and water that flowed with the same forgiveness we receive today in Word and Sacrament. Several famous works of church art, such as the 1555 altarpiece painting in the Church of Sts. Peter and Paul in Weimar, Germany, depict the crucifixion, including this particular event, in an allegorical way. Instead of reproducing what the scene would have looked like, these pictures sometimes include a person who was really not there (for instance, Martin Luther), and then you see that a stream of blood issuing from Jesus' side is landing on that person's head. The message is intended to say that this person, even though he wasn't physically there, made a clear confession of faith during his lifetime. He admitted his own sinfulness and placed his complete trust in the blood of Christ to cleanse his soul and make him perfectly clean and righteous.

So Zechariah did not miss a beat, when, after writing about the One who was pierced, he continued with the fountain that was opened from that holy wound for the citizens of New Jerusalem, the Church. The day of the Lord's grace, inaugurated on Good Friday and proclaimed ever since the first Easter, means cleansing from every sin and uncleanness for all who hear His Word and believe in His salvation. The prophet paints a picture not only of forgiveness but also of the total eradication of sin. Both are necessary, because one gift would have been worthless for the Christian believer without the other. The death of Jesus Christ would be treated with utter contempt if it were used in order to keep evil fires burning. "I don't have to worry about sin. I can just ask for forgiveness!" May that attitude never entice us!

The two examples of sanctification that Zechariah addressed are two sins that are especially damaging to faith, namely, idolatry and false prophecy. Idols were to be removed. Even their names were to be completely eradicated. We read passages like that today and say, "Well, that's easy enough! Just destroy those statues of wood, bronze, and gold, and you can cross that off your to-do list!" But idolatry, as we know from our own human nature, is more than just bowing down to a graven image. It is trusting in anything else besides God. Idolatry attacks when we worry about something, even though our heavenly Father has already taken care of it. Idolatry is refusing to pray to the Lord but meditating instead on how this or that person has hurt us and we can't wait to return the "favor."

False prophecy was a big problem in Israel and Judah in the generations leading up to the Assyrian invasion and the Babylonian exile. It worked hand-in-hand with idolatry and the worship of the gods of neighboring countries. False prophets were like regular government employees in the days of evil kings such as Ahab. He needed them to tell him what he wanted to hear, because the genuine prophets were telling him only bad news. Some impostors dressed up in cloaks of hair in order to look like a true prophet, such as Elijah. So now that the exile was over and people were resettling the Holy Land, Zechariah was assuring this new generation that even parents of a false prophet would not stand for his deception. They would rather condemn their own son, even piercing him through themselves, than allow the truth to be contradicted. If that seems too extreme, then consider the words of our Lord Jesus Christ: (Luke 14:26) "If anyone comes to Me and does not hate his own father and mother and wife and children and brothers and sisters, yes, and even his own life, he cannot be My disciple."

4 Strike the Shepherd (Zechariah 13:7–9)

(Luke 24:7) "The Son of Man must be delivered into the hands of sinful men." Jesus Himself stated the message of Scripture concerning His destiny on the cross. People will sin against Jesus, and yet in a strange way, they did Him a favor as He accomplished our salvation. This irony is present in the entire story from Judas's betrayal on Maundy Thursday to the Roman soldiers' false report on Easter. God manipulates the evil of mankind to become His goodness toward all believers.

The sword of judgment is awakened at the Lord's command, but instead of being wielded against the sheep who have sinned against God, this sword pierced the Shepherd. Jesus is the man who stands next to God the Father in the glory He has shared from before creation. The Holy Trinity is coequal in majesty, as the Bible makes clear in both Old and New Testaments. Jesus also stands next to God the Father in moral purity, since in His human nature He was the only one who completely fulfilled the will of God as it is taught and presented in the Ten Commandments.

The sword of judgment originally intended for the sheep strikes the Shepherd instead. This means a substitution, an atonement, is accomplished—a sufficient price has been paid to satisfy the wrath of God and the wages of sin. He was struck down not in a forgettable skirmish with nitpicking religious officials, not in a remote back alley by a faceless mob, but just outside the most important city in Palestine, on the occasion of a Passover festival that drew many witnesses. It was the sword of fully authorized justice that cut Him down. Our Lord was crucified as a criminal, even though Pontius Pilate, acting as mouthpiece for God the Father, declared Him fully innocent.

Zechariah was allowed to preview the famous Garden of Gethsemane scene with Judas betraying Jesus with a kiss and then engaging the other disciples in a tussle that ended with our Lord arrested and the disciples running away. Just as the prophet said, (v. 7) "Strike the shepherd, and the sheep will be scattered."

That's hardly a glorious picture of the Church's victory. Yet through the lens of Christ's cross, it is precisely through suffering that God's chosen saints persevere to life everlasting. They may not be many, but a remnant, as we found out at the beginning of this study, was never meant to be large. Zechariah describes the Church in three "bites," or mouthfuls. Two of the three bites are cut off, and they are gone, leaving the last. This portion, even though God has promised them prosperity in the end, would first suffer all kinds of trials, crosses, and tribulations, as though they were gold and silver being heated in a furnace. When this little, cross-stricken remnant calls on the Lord in their time of trouble, He promises to answer them and deliver them, and they will glorify Him by voicing the simple confession: (v. 9) "The Lord is my God."

5 King over All the Earth (Zechariah 14)

Tribulation, persecution, and struggle are still prescribed for the Jerusalem of the future, which from our perspective is better known as the Holy Christian Church. The Lord desires for His people to withstand these tests of faith and emerge all the stronger for it. Yet enemies will still mount their attacks throughout the Church's history, and earthly spoils will be plundered from God's children. Cities will be attacked, people will be killed, and worldly possessions will be dispossessed, all in an attempt to snatch what the forces of evil can never steal away. Even though in the back of our minds we shudder to think what we would do if such devastation were to happen to us, we know with confidence that even then, our Lord has not given up on us. He will see us through to the finish line.

Imagine our mighty God emerging on the horizon like a huge colossus, stepping over mountain ranges as though they were speed bumps! Zechariah wrote of this dramatic divine appearance, depicting the Lord of hosts standing over Jerusalem like a giant, His feet stomping down just outside the borders of the city on the Mount of Olives. His footprint shoves the terrain north and south as it carves a new valley out of the seemingly immovable hill, revealing the largest ever escape slide leading from the high-elevation Jerusalem down to the Jordan River valley, also known as the Arabah. Zechariah chose to describe a heavenly scene concerning the Church using the geography that was familiar to him. In the same way, we explain Jesus' parables as earthly stories with a heavenly meaning. The appearance of God as a giant, creating an exit ramp through the mountain, teaches us that for faithful believers, there will be a place to flee from the attacks they will suffer. The Lord Himself will provide the way of escape.

Following that miraculous escape, the prophet bids his hearers to look forward to a truly unique day, a day without light, cold, or frost, and it could be called neither day nor night. This is a new creation, a dawning of eternity that coincides with the arrival of our Savior in His full, heavenly glory. The image of water flowing out from Jerusalem is not unique to Zechariah. The Books of Ezekiel and Revelation also depict a stream that grants life and refreshment to all who seek it from the Lord. But here we witness a forked stream going in two directions, east and west. The spread of God's Word for the salvation of all nations will cover all the earth until all those, whom the Lord alone knows, hear and believe.

The final image of God's vindication for His Church is the Feast of Booths (or Tabernacles). Celebrated at harvesttime, this Jewish feast included living in tents to remind the people of the exodus long ago and how the Lord took care of His people and fulfilled His promises to them. Our Church Year calendar may no longer include the Festival of Booths, but right about harvesttime there is the theme of the last days and Christ's coming to judge all nations. In a fitting coincidence, the American Day of Thanksgiving usually occurs at about the same time. When our Savior returns, everything that has ever threatened to destroy us will be swept away forever. We will stand before our Lord, completely and eternally purged of our old sinful natures, covered in the righteousness of Jesus, and be welcomed into God's radiant presence forever. Then will be the time for endless thanksgiving.

Conclusion

Ezra wrote that Zechariah helped the people rebuild the temple in Jerusalem. We have seen, especially in the latter chapters of his book, that Zechariah was inspired by the Holy Spirit to set his sights on a greater establishment, the Church of our Lord and Savior Jesus Christ. He not only predicted specific events of Jesus' suffering and death but also pointed the faithful to the life of the world to come.

Concluding Activities

Conclude the session with an appropriate prayer and distribute the study leaflet for week 8.

Malachi, My Messenger

Malachi 1–2

Preparing for the Session

Central Focus

Malachi is the final prophet to write before the arrival of Jesus, even though there is a period of four hundred years between the events. He is particularly interested in purifying the corrupt worship practices of the priests and strengthening the covenant of love that the Lord had established with His chosen people. Soon, all nations will participate in the plan of salvation, so God's people will need to rededicate themselves to their holy purpose as a light to the Gentiles.

Objectives

That participants, led by the Holy Spirit working through God's Word, will

1. identify the main areas in Israel's life in which Malachi calls God's people to repentance;
2. understand the connections Malachi makes between ceremony and faith; and
3. give thanks to the Lord for His steadfast love and covenant faithfulness to us.

Note for the small-group leaders: Lesson notes and other materials you will need begin on page 81.

For the Lecture Leader

Session Plan

Worship

Begin the session with the hymn printed in the study leaflet. Accompaniments are available in denominational hymnals, such as *Lutheran Service Book* or *Lutheran Worship* (refer to hymnal index). (Note: Concordia Publishing House has available *The Concordia Organist*. All the initial worship hymns in the LifeLight courses are included in this resource. It's especially helpful for mission congregations and small parishes. See the list of study resources on p. 7.) Follow with this prayer:

Prayer

Heavenly Father, guard our lips with Your saving knowledge. You have abundantly showered us with blessings. You have honored Your promises and remained faithful to us, even though we have disobeyed You in thought, word, and deed. Before our sins harden our hearts and seriously damage our relationship with You, grant us repentance, forgiveness, and purification by Your Word. Bind us to You in the marriage covenant of faith, so that we may look forward with expectant joy as we await the second coming of our Messiah, Jesus, in whose name we pray. Amen.

Lecture Presentation

1 Jacob versus Esau (Malachi 1:1–5)

"Mom always loved you more!" When children surmise in their parents' attitudes even the hint of playing favorites, a sibling rivalry can easily turn into a costly war. The smile of a mother toward one child is twisted into a conspiracy in the mind of a brother or sister who happens to see it. What makes it even worse is when the child who seems to be in the position of the favorite begins to expect and demand *more* of the attention and favor. Then one success after another in this matter yields the result for which no one likes to claim responsibility: a spoiled child.

Malachi arrived on the prophetic scene when Judah and the inhabitants of Jerusalem were throwing one of their tantrums, claiming the Lord didn't really love them. They defiantly challenged their heavenly Father, spitting His claims of love and favor right back in His face. God's people demanded that He show them more evidence that He would fulfill His promises toward them. They refused to acknowledge that, for centuries, the Lord had been faithful to His chosen people. The prophet Malachi, whose name means "My messenger" or possibly "Messenger of the Lord," was instructed to point out a well-known episode in Israel's history—the divine preference of Jacob over Esau: (vv. 2–3) "Yet I have loved Jacob but Esau I have hated." See there?! What further proof do you need of God playing favorites? Even though Esau was the older one of the twins, Jacob was given the promise that the Lord originally bequeathed to their grandfather Abraham. The rivalry between the two began in the womb—they were constantly wrestling and struggling to the point of driving Rebekah, their mother, to ask the Lord what was going on. This was the struggle of whole nations against each other. Both will become great peoples, but only one will have the favored status as bearer of the Messiah's family line. As the Lord Himself said to their mother long ago: (Genesis 25:23) "the older shall serve the younger," so His great promises and favors would be granted to Jacob's descendants instead of Esau's. God did not "hate" Esau in the sense that he was excluded from salvation. The phrase was spoken specifically to people of Israel, and God meant it as a comparison to the abundant grace He had granted to the ones who have the rights to His inheritance. Earlier, we recalled that Jesus required us to "hate" our family members in the sense of making them second to Him. So also here in Malachi, God wants to affirm His love to skeptical Judah by pointing out how the children of Jacob's closest relative, Esau, were not going to receive a fraction of the blessings they themselves have. Their ingratitude is entirely unfounded.

Even though Esau was the apparent favorite of his father, Isaac, he didn't seem to have the same confident faith. His hunting skills earned him some privileges, but when he was unsuccessful and his hunger made him think that he was on the verge of death, Esau despised his birthright and sold it to Jacob for a single meal of red stew. Jacob, with the help of his mother, deceived Isaac and stole the birthright blessing, so Esau was forced away from the vicinity of the Promised Land. His descendants after him, those who became the nation of Edom, lived most of the time as wanderers. Their history would be replete with destruction, their land would be laid waste, and their great cities would be shattered ruins. God even commanded that if they decide to rebuild, He would vow to tear it down. As a testament to the Lord's love for His chosen people, the ones to whom the Messiah would come, and in order to prompt their praise of His power even beyond their own borders, He would saddle their wicked kinsmen the Edomites with the shameful name (v. 4) "the people with whom the Lord is angry forever."

2 Polluted Food (Malachi 1:6–10)

The Lord's words of disgust have now turned to His priests serving in the temple. By the time Malachi began his prophetic ministry, the temple had been completely rebuilt, and Nehemiah had finished the Jerusalem city wall. Sacrifices were back in the routine of the Israelites, and the "routine" of it all may have been part of their problem. Obeying God's holy commands and following His order of worship had become a despised routine and a chore. No gratitude was expressed in their offerings; they were concerned only about cutting corners and going through the motions.

Malachi was instrumental in shining the light of truth on a new kind of idolatry that was more subtle than what got the people of God in trouble before the Babylonian exile. Back then, the offense was more overt—statues were made, altars were built, and the people intentionally avoided every ceremony that Moses commanded in favor of what they had come up with in their own minds. Now that the people had returned to Jerusalem, rebuilt the temple, and more fully repopulated the area, they had promised to Ezra and Nehemiah to worship only the Lord and to dedicate themselves to His commandments and ceremonies. It didn't take long, though, and their religious fervor degenerated into a mere show of piety. To the casual observer who knew nothing about the divine rules, what they were doing looked pretty good. But this false show of worship was just as bad as (if not worse than) the previous gross displays of idolatry, because it was easier to excuse their laziness and lack of faith as though they were perfectly following the Lord's Word.

And the challenges kept coming. The accused priests fired right back at God: (v. 6) "How have we despised Your name?" They were confident that they could hide behind their less-than-par substitutions for sacrifices and nobody would notice—yes, they even expected the Lord to count their insult as a high honor! But the Lord's words, using Malachi's unique style, fire the questions right back, cutting them deep with precision analogies that clearly reveal their rebellious attitude. A son is commanded to honor his father, and instead of flatly stating, "You don't honor me," God asks the pointed question, "If I am a father, where is My honor?" The point of the rhetorical question was "It just isn't there!" because there was no example they could point to. These priests had no fear of divine punishment for their actions—the height of arrogance.

In verses 7–8, we read the incriminating facts: these priests were offering polluted food on the altar. "Food" here means sacrifices dedicated to the Lord, whether offerings of animals or grain. "Polluted" was a term of ceremonial disqualification for several reasons: meat with blood left in it, blemished and diseased animals, inedible grain that was suitable only for the trash heap or manure pile. When these horribly substandard offerings were put forward in gross disobedience to the Lord's liturgical directions, they were condemned by Malachi as evil. Even though he was merely the representative of Persia who had only temporal power over them, they would not have insulted him the way they had slighted the Lord of heaven and earth! In other words, "With offerings like these, who needs offenses?" That's why the Lord had Malachi suggest that they just close the doors and stop sacrificing at the temple altogether. According to Him, what they were doing would not be recognized in the sight of God.

3 The Lord and the Leftovers (Malachi 1:11–14)

The eyes of the Lord are not so nearsighted as to pay attention just to Jerusalem and a handful of priests who were disobeying Him. His sights were set on a much wider perspective: (v. 11) "From the rising of the sun to its setting My name will be great among the nations." Their insulting worship practices were impacting not only their local situation, but they were also abysmal failures in their role as a light for the Messiah to all nations. When the Lord's name was profaned, it had effects far beyond Israel's earthly borders.

Other nations would see that God's own people despised His abundant grace. Outsiders would have never treated their own gods with such disrespect as the Hebrews were doing, so how could anyone expect to convince the idolaters that they were not worshiping the one true God? On the contrary, in the Lord's master plan for the Holy Christian Church, the time would come when the tables would be turned and He would accept the worship of true faith in Christ as it comes from all corners of the earth. Gentiles around the world would soon extol the Lord with the incense of prayers in the name of Jesus and the pure offerings of good works performed because of His grace.

Meanwhile, the privileged people of God, beginning at the top with their priests, who should have known better, were making the holy seem worthless and common. That is what profaning the name of the Lord really means—treating a holy treasure as though it were a filthy rag. It doesn't necessarily have to do with profanity, as in bad language; rather, it desecrates that which is sacred.

Yet these priests continued to feel no shame. When confronted with the truth, they were not humbled to repentance. They made no point to reverse their subtle form of idolatry. In fact, to take it in the other direction—these malefactors made themselves out to be the victims! They made it seem like all these rules for worship conduct were weighing them down and cramping their style: (v. 13) "What a weariness this is," so they snort, "God is just being unreasonable—He's exasperating us with His persnickety regulations!" They were caught offering stolen animals and maimed specimens and encouraging cheats to use the worst for a gift of thanksgiving to God when they had the best ready and waiting. Even though they were clearly shown to be in the wrong, they always had an excuse: God cannot possibly expect us to be so perfect as to offer Him our best at all times, could He?

Yes, He does expect something from His dear children. In the Old Testament, He demanded pure sacrifices so that the temple rituals revealed to the whole world what Jesus was going to come and do for all. They had a job, a calling in life, you could say, to keep up those sacrifices day after day until all those offerings finally came to fulfillment in Christ. The Jewish leaders were called on to stop their self-serving practices and turn all attention to the Lord's mercy.

In the New Testament, which includes our own day, the Lord's expectations are only slightly different. Instead of demanding the former ceremonies of sacrifices and feasts, He calls on all baptized royal priests of God in Christ to live in their new calling as Christians. He desires faith in the forgiveness of sins to reign supreme in their hearts, followed by good works that lead others to see what faith can do in the life of God's people. Because of that, they will praise the Father in heaven (Matthew 5:16).

4 The Lips of the Priest (Malachi 2:1–9)

Malachi was not moved by the Holy Spirit to reveal any specific details about himself. Most prophets opened their books with identifying information—for instance, Ezekiel's introduction is quite detailed and autobiographical: (Ezekiel 1:1–3) "In the thirtieth year, in the fourth month, on the fifth day of the month, as I was among the exiles by the Chebar canal, the heavens were opened, and I saw visions of God. On the fifth day of the month (it was the fifth year of the exile of King Jehoiachin), the word of the Lord came to Ezekiel the priest, the son of Buzi, in the land of the Chaldeans by the Chebar canal, and the hand of the LORD was upon him there." No doubt there about who, what, when, and where! Malachi, on the other hand, gives only his name in the first verse of his book. Nothing else shows up about him, whether you're talking about his fifty-four other verses in the book that bears his name or anywhere else in Holy Scripture.

One thing about Malachi, however, that you may notice: he is focused intently on the members of the tribe of Levi in general and the priests of the Lord in particular. Whether that definitively places him on the inside as a fellow Levite, or even a priest, is anyone's guess. The Lord could certainly call on anyone to speak His Word of warning to this special class of Israelites. No matter what tribe or family they may have hailed from, all faithful members of God's chosen nation would have been keenly aware of how much they depended on a pure priesthood. This handful of men served their countrymen as mediators of the Lord's covenant, teachers of His Holy Law, and mouthpieces of divine blessing.

Whether or not he had seen these worship abuses as an insider, Malachi unleashed a scathing rebuke against the priests, who by their reprehensible actions had refused to give honor to the name of the Lord. They would not be able to escape the curse He had threatened. Whenever they pronounced blessings, God would make them into curses. Whenever these wicked priests would perform the animal sacrifices, the unusable, waste portions that normally were cut out of the animal, separated from the part that was the offering, and burned in the trash heap—this so-called "dung" would be smeared in disgusting disgrace all over their faces. Even their offspring will bear their fathers' curse and humiliation. Yet in all of this mess and devastation, the Lord would still keep His covenant of life and peace that He originally made with their ancestor Levi, the son of Jacob.

Even if the servants of the Lord, who are handing out the heavenly treasures in His stead, were found to be unworthy, corrupt, and godless, that still could not nullify the grace-filled arrangement set up at Mount Sinai a thousand years before Malachi wrote. The Word of God is still the Word of God and carries with it God's promise of forgiveness and everlasting life, even when an absolute scoundrel might be holding the office and preaching the Word. Jesus Himself in Matthew 23:2 told people to listen to His enemies, the scribes and Pharisees, because they "sit on Moses' seat," that is, they were the ones to whom the Lord gave His authority and responsibility, even though they themselves did not practice what they preached.

Even so, the priests in Malachi's day were charged with an obligation to teach: (2:7) "The lips of a priest should guard knowledge." That vivid image succinctly describes their great responsibility. Ministers of God's Word are not called to make people stumble. They will be held accountable. They must do all they can to impart not just any old knowledge—their hearers need the knowledge of salvation in Jesus Christ. That message of the Gospel is what makes the minister—whether prophet, priest, apostle, or pastor—a holy messenger of the Lord of hosts.

5 Married in God's Eyes (Malachi 2:10–17)

(V. 10) "Have we not all one Father?" You can almost hear the endless repetition of the song "It's a small world after all." But Malachi was not exactly making that point with his question. For one thing, if he was about to make the case that everybody in the world is the same, no matter what their background, then he would not have, in the verses immediately following, proceeded to criticize the Jews for marrying a daughter of a foreign god! This practice was an abomination against the God who was Israel's Father—the source of all their good—because of His covenant of grace made with Abraham, their forefather.

The ancient covenant itself was also being desecrated, profaned, because "we" have been faithless to one another. This was Malachi including himself in the call to repentance! He was not trying to claim responsibility for someone else's sin. Instead, he was highlighting how the community was "all in this together" when sin plagues the entire fellowship. We can see this as true for ourselves as well. We get nowhere by blaming the sinners, pointing them out for ridicule and hoping that the consequences of their sin won't affect us too much. If we are bound together in one covenant with God and with our brothers and sisters in Christ, then when one part suffers, all parts suffer together with it.

But why was marriage causing all these problems? God's people were integrating with the societies all around them. They were no longer an isolated nation, like in the time of Kings David and Solomon when they had been prosperous all on their own without the influence of outside empires. Now, in Malachi's day, there was a Persian Empire to the north and east, and Greece was swiftly taking over the reins of power in the west. By the time Jesus was born, the Roman Empire had replaced both of those. The people may well have argued that times had changed and intermarriage was unavoidable—you couldn't expect Israel to turn back the clock to the way things were before the exile!

God was not impressed by that plea. He still presented His case against those who had married foreign women. Since He also mentioned (v. 15) "the wife of your youth," it is likely that many of the people of Judah had divorced their believing first spouses and then married pagans who would not change to the religion of the one true God. This is the historical context for what is an often-quoted verse: (v. 16 NKJV) "For the LORD God of Israel says That He hates divorce." This is not referring to the divorce that God allows for a deserted spouse to protect him or herself (see 1 Corinthians 7:15) or in cases of adultery (Matthew 19:9). This was instead using divorce in order to break a promise to a fellow believer, as well as breaking faith with God Himself by welcoming pagan beliefs into their homes. The Israelites were not to open the door so much as a crack if there would be a risk that false faith could enter and infect the Israelite home. This certainly tells us loud and clear, (v. 16) "Guard yourselves in your spirit, and do not be faithless."

Conclusion

Malachi announced strong rebukes from the Lord's judgment throne against corrupt priests and those residents of Judah who simultaneously had broken their marriage vows and their faith with God. He used rhetorical questions to spur their repentance and did not hold back when informing them of the consequences of their sins. The prophet has therefore set the stage for his prophecy's main feature: the promised Messiah, whose prophecies we will read about in our next session.

Concluding Activities

Conclude the session with an appropriate prayer and distribute the study leaflet for week 9.

The Coming Messenger
Malachi 3–4

Preparing for the Session

Central Focus

Malachi's final prophetic messages are meant to inspire faith among the people living in the newly rebuilt Judah and Jerusalem. He departs from the topic of priestly corruption to highlight the coming of the promised Messenger and those who would prepare ahead of Him. After he urges repentance on a faithless and selfish nation, Malachi promises a great and final day of salvation for believers but destruction for the wicked.

Objectives

That participants, led by the Holy Spirit working through God's Word, will

1. perceive the need for repentance when their lives reflect a lack of faith;
2. look forward joyfully to the continuous coming of the Savior for forgiveness; and
3. be encouraged to continue studying the Bible and discover more of its riches!

Note for the small-group leaders: Lesson notes and other materials you will need begin on page 84.

For the Lecture Leader

Session Plan

Worship

Begin the session with the hymn printed in the study leaflet. Accompaniments are available in denominational hymnals, such as *Lutheran Service Book* or *Lutheran Worship* (refer to hymnal index). (Note: Concordia Publishing House has available *The Concordia Organist.* All the initial worship hymns in the LifeLight courses are included in this resource. It's especially helpful for mission congregations and small parishes. See the list of study resources on p. 7.) Follow with this prayer:

Prayer

Almighty and eternal God and Father, You have promised everlasting life to us in Jesus Christ, our Savior. You have sent us prophets and apostles and messengers to proclaim Your Word to us and turn our hearts to You in repentance. Forgive us when we have not shown a strong faith in You through our gifts, tithes, and hearts. Open Your book of remembrance and record our names for now and for eternity, especially since we have not done anything to deserve Your favor, but Jesus has granted us His heavenly inheritance. Heal us under Your wings and let the sun of Your grace shine with Your abundant pardon, so that we may not be put to shame but rather leap with joy for all that You have done for us. In the name of Jesus we pray. Amen.

Lecture Presentation

1 The Messenger Will Purify (Malachi 3:1–5)

In Malachi 2:17, the prophet rebuked the people, "You have wearied the Lord with your words." How could God become weary or tired? We learned from Genesis that the Lord God rested on the seventh day after He created the heavens and the earth. As children, we may have asked, "Why did God rest? Was He tired?" I had thought it was obvious that He didn't need to recover energy after six days of work, but that He created and blessed a Sabbath because He knew we would need a day of rest and worship.

But in 2:17, we find God weary, just as you and I become weary. He has had enough! Though at first they did not want to own up to it, God's chosen people are accusing their Lord of gross injustice. And He did not want to hear it anymore. The alleged unfairness is this: "Everyone who does evil is good in the sight of the Lord, and He delights in them." The bad guys get off scot-free! The wicked prosper! How dare our God act apparently against His own promises! They did not simply fault the Lord with a brief lapse of justice; they are actually so bold as to question His very existence: "Where is the God of justice?"

Little did these faithless complainers realize that the almighty God was setting in motion His most important piece of the salvation puzzle. The promised Savior was on His way, but first He would send a messenger to prepare hearts to welcome Him. Malachi was the messenger designated to be the last one to write before the Old Testament came to an end. John the Baptist would be the prophet of the Most High, appointed to signal the end of the Old Testament at that moment he points with his finger to Jesus and says, (John 1:29) "Behold, the Lamb of God, who takes away the sin of the world!"

For Jesus, the Messenger above all Messengers, the Angel of the Lord, would finally arrive on earth in flesh and blood, the baby born of the Virgin Mary in the little town of Bethlehem. He would suddenly come to His temple—not merely the building but also the temple of His human body (John 2:21). But will His coming be as frightening as Malachi warns? He says, (v. 2) "Who can endure . . . who can stand when He appears?" Indeed, our Lord's first coming was not for condemnation of the ungodly, but for salvation. Yet His work of mankind's salvation did involve a battle against the evil forces that opposed Him, although it was largely a hidden, spiritual battle. When Jesus was killed on the cross, it looked as though He was defeated in shame. In reality, that was His highest triumph over hell and Satan. Neither the devil nor his entire evil host will be able to stand.

Forgiveness, earned by the blood of Christ, will purify a new generation of priests. This is the New Testament order of priests who are consecrated by the water of Baptism. All Christian believers are royal priests, and Jesus, the Lord of hosts in human flesh, has purified us and refined us like gold and silver. Those who formerly were wicked sinners are now fully good and perfect in the sight of God. This is not to encourage His people to keep on doing evil (see Romans 6:1–2), but the Gospel is a free gift of God's favor toward sinners. When the final judgment comes, those who are hardened, faithless evildoers will face utter condemnation. The Lord Himself will testify against them, saying, (Matthew 7:23) "I never knew you." Those who believe will be a lovely and fragrant offering to the Lord, full of righteousness and pleasant in His sight, just like at the beginning.

2 Will Man Rob God? (Malachi 3:6–11)

If your concept of God is based solely on your daily experience in this fallen world, you could easily see Him as capricious, vengeful, unforgiving, and even a bit touchy at times. God's Law might as well be the same as Murphy's Law. With a god like that, you would do nothing but complain that you can't get ahead, that the deck is stacked against you. Your religious actions would consist of one attempt after another to try and pacify this always-angry, never-satisfied god. What do I have to do *now* to catch a break? The idea of karma is not limited to Hinduism—it stands for a dream that is stuck in the sinful, fallen human mind because our earthly experiences seem to tell us that life is unfair, that justice will finally shake things out in the end. Some believe that if we work hard enough at doing what we think is good, and if we are patient, then maybe a little good will come back our way. Many people, including many Christians, have made their religion into something like this: "Do whatever you think will earn you more good than bad. All things considered, you can only trust yourself."

We need Holy Scripture to tell us who the true God is. We cannot go on our daily experiences alone, because all that we experience in this world is tainted by sin. Ever since Adam and Eve, Satan has succeeded in convincing human beings to trust in their own hearts and feelings and doubt the love of our Father in heaven. It should be the other way around. The Bible, understood not as a book of rules but as revealing God's mercy in Jesus Christ, gives the only perfect picture of our Lord as He has made Himself known to the creatures He so dearly loves. Contrary to what your experiences tell you, (v. 6) "I the LORD do not change." He will always help and strengthen you, even when you look all around and think that you are on your own.

Malachi began his book by recalling the story of Jacob and Esau. His point was that history actually demonstrates that the Lord had shown great love to His chosen people. Investment advisers are obligated to tell us something like this: "Past performance does not necessarily indicate future results." There is always the risk that something terrible will happen and we will lose everything. Not so with the track record of the almighty God! He has come through in the past, so you can be assured that He will always be at your side to save you. Take comfort that you are the spiritual children of Jacob, the one who was loved, instead of the despised and faithless Esau. Your spiritual father Jacob may have been a deceiver and imperfect character (Genesis 27:35–36), but he stood for all of us unworthy sinners who have received the undeserved mercy of our heavenly Father.

So God calls us to put His love to the test! Wait, what did He say? I thought it was forbidden to test God! No, this is a test of your own faith. Will you believe that the Lord loves you and wants to bless you? The children of Jacob have for too long assumed, along with the rest of the sinful world, that they have to wait for karma to reward them. "Not so," says the Lord. "Do what I command you, that is, believe in Me and trust that even when you give back in your tithe part of what I have provided you, still you will have no lack. Convince yourself that all of what you have is actually My gift to you, and then you will rejoice in My richest abundance."

3 Blessings from All Nations (Malachi 3:12–15)

In chapter 3, the prophet Malachi renewed his concern over the witness of God's chosen people, Israel. All the other peoples of the world still had their attention focused on the Holy Land. Back in chapter 1, the issue was "Would the foreign nations see a holy people destroyed because they despised God's name?" That put the matter in a negative light; it was designed to wake up the lackadaisical descendants of Abraham so that they would not get themselves swept away—yet again. Particular attention had to be directed toward the priests and their attitude toward their holy tasks of sacrifices and atonement.

This time, the thrust is quite a bit more positive. After the Lord rebukes the people for robbing God in the withholding of their tithes, you might think that we are going down the road of more threats and punishments. But suddenly, there is an unexpected turn. Israel's God actually invites the people to test Him and give their full, previously promised tithe, then step back and get ready for the abundance that will flood back to them in return! It sounds like a pretty good deal—sacrifice a portion of the best now in a gift that you are to give back to the Lord, and later you will receive a bumper crop of blessings, chief among them being life everlasting. As Jesus promises to those who reflect the forgiving and giving nature of their heavenly Father, the harvest of God's good things is described this way: (Luke 6:38) "Good measure, pressed down, shaken together, running over, will be put into your lap."

And that is what the other nations would see. Instead of witnessing Israel or a Church in disarray because the people seem to have no more use for God, unbelievers will see a prosperity not necessarily measured by the standards of the world. In believers, they will witness a contentment that most definitely is foreign to contemporary society. Whether I have much or I have little, I have the Lord Jesus Christ, and that is my greatest treasure. If anything will make the other nations talk, it will be that! And our Lord Himself knew this to be true—that is why He told His disciples, (Matthew 5:16) "Let your light shine before others, so that they may see your good works and give glory to your Father who is in heaven." Good deeds, God-given abundance, and Gospel words of forgiveness are the triple crown of an effective witness to the true faith in this fallen, sinful world.

But perhaps we just are not seeing this rich abundance that we hear about! We may struggle to pay bills. We may find ourselves in conflicts at home, work, or school. We may not feel prosperous at all. Fear not! You are in good company if you feel that way. Malachi's hearers also grumbled that it seemed totally vain—an utterly useless proposition—to serve God. Why should we go about in solemn piety and look to others like we are in mourning? If the Lord forgives all sinners, then why should we be constantly under pressure to keep from sinning? Those evildoers out there are getting all the prosperity we should have for ourselves! They are unfettered with rules and regulations from on high. We look with desperate longing at those extra hours that everybody else has on Sunday mornings, while we are busy scurrying to park our back sides in the church pew! That's not the testing that the Lord had in mind! He still requires your trust in Him that He will truly provide—and He most certainly will.

4 Remembered in God's Book (Malachi 3:16–18)

We recalled earlier in Session 4 that Noah's fortunes took a positive turn when the inspired narrator records the pivotal verse: (Genesis 8:1) "But God remembered Noah." The point behind saying that He "remembered" is that God had made a promise, and the fulfillment was about to take place. As the wall of Jerusalem was being rebuilt and several reforms were needed, the hardworking Nehemiah pleaded, (Nehemiah 13:31) "Remember me, O my God, for good." When the word "remember" is used about God, it usually refers to the hopeful end of an extended period of waiting for His Word to come true.

The Bible also discusses a book of remembrance in which the names of the believers, the saints, are written. Of course, the Lord has no need of any written record in order to prevent Him from forgetting. That would be what earthly rulers need, such as the Persian King Xerxes (a.k.a. Ahasuerus) in Esther 6. He not only required the records to prove a certain deed was done in the king's favor, but he also thought the dry, repetitive minutes of throne-room sessions would surely cure his insomnia! Instead, the image of the heavenly record book that is mentioned here, in the Psalms, and in the Book of Revelation, is meant to grant assurance to believers that neither (Romans 8:39) "height nor depth, nor anything else in all creation, will be able to separate us from the love of God in Christ Jesus our Lord." Having your name written in the Lord's book is further confirmation that you have been saved by grace, through faith, by means of the saving death and resurrection of Jesus.

In depicting what will happen to the faithful on the Day of Judgment, Malachi quoted the Lord as He explained what the names in the book mean. They denote the ones who truly fear the Lord, the ones who esteem His name. The appearance of the name in the book ultimately means what our Savior has said: They shall be Mine. I will gather them up as My treasured possession. It will not be due to anything that they have done, but by grace these sinners will be spared just like a father spares his beloved son. This beautiful guarantee will later be rephrased in the mouth of Jesus Himself with another figure of speech: (John 10:14, 27, 28) "I am the good shepherd. . . . My sheep hear My voice, and I know them. . . . No one will snatch them out of My hand."

5 Elijah Preparing the Way (Malachi 4)

The day when the Lord claims His treasured possession as His own and spares those who serve Him is the same Day of Judgment during which He will unleash burning fury against the arrogant and the evildoers. This is where the concepts of Law and Gospel, condemnation and forgiveness, in the writings of the prophets heighten to their greatest contrast. What will be in store for those whom the Lord loves and forgives? They will be relieved from their sorrows and preserved from everlasting condemnation. And for the enemies of God? Nothing will be left of them but scorched earth where they once stood, and the righteous will stomp in victory on their ashes.

When the Lord told Moses and later Joshua to wipe out a certain city or people, He commanded them to devote them to utter destruction. They were cursed under God's righteous judgment, and He wanted His chosen people to carry out the decree of His ban. On the great final day of His coming, God's people will get to see how He would do it Himself. When He sent the plagues on Egypt in the time of Moses, the Lord made a distinction between the Egyptians and the Israelites. While devastation ravaged the country, the only place untouched by harm was Goshen, where God's people were staying. When deepest darkness crippled Pharaoh and his people, there was light shining for those who were listening to God's Word through Moses. And when the angel of death robbed every Egyptian household of its firstborn son, those who faithfully observed the first Passover were spared.

So wherever destruction, judgment, and God's holy anger is threatened against stubborn sinfulness, He graciously provides a way for faithful, humble, and repentant people to believe in His grace and find their way of escape. Malachi identifies that conduit to the Lord's mercy as Elijah the prophet, a powerful preacher of repentance (fulfilled in John the Baptist, see Matthew 11:12–14), whom God would send to turn hearts of fathers to their children and the hearts of children to their fathers. One generation usually thinks it can outdo the other in just about anything. But when a heritage of faith and full trust in God's promises of salvation is passed from one generation to the next, it is a miracle wrought by the work of the Holy Spirit.

We have previously pondered how a Good Friday service can be a memorable and meaningful proclamation of our Lord's holy death. Another service that sticks in the minds of many people is the Easter sunrise service. The eager early risers drag their half-asleep family members into the church, pointing out the beautiful decorations and Easter lilies. The darkness outside has not yet subsided, and the chill in the air adds to the excitement. If the service time works out just right, the piercing light of the sun meets the faces of the congregation just as they hear the infinitely brighter Gospel of forgiveness of sins, resurrection of the body, and life everlasting in the risen Lord Jesus Christ. Many churches have either their altars or their front doors facing to the east, partly because of Malachi. In his final chapter, he depicted the Messiah as the (v. 2) "sun of righteousness," who rises up like the dawn with healing in His wings. What better time is there in the Church Year than the service during which there is featured both the resurrection of our

Savior and the expectation of the sunrise? Facing east is yet another symbol of expectant faith in Him who has promised to come again soon.

Conclusion

Malachi was inspired to bring the Old Testament era of written prophecy to a close with several topics, each handled briefly. He recorded the promised coming of a messenger in the power of Elijah to prepare the way for a greater Messenger of the covenant who will come to His temple. The prophet chastened his fellow Israelites of robbing God but challenged them to trust in His generous providence. And he lauded the coming of the great and final day of the Lord in which both judgment and mercy will find utter completeness. God's people were given four hundred years to consider his words and the rest of Scripture before Christ finally arrived. We have much to study ourselves as we prepare for Him to come again!

This prophecy was recorded and preserved by God's providence so that we, too, would read these tremendous words warning and of promise. For we, too, look for and long for Christ's return as people in the dark of night long for the coming of the dawn. Through Malachi, we know for certain that the night that is life in this fallen world is not endless—the dawn will come. Indeed, our Lord will return, as He promised. On that great and awesome day, Jesus, the very Sun of righteousness, will arise over the world to make all things new and gather us around the glory of His presence forever.

Concluding Activities

Conclude the session with an appropriate prayer and announce the next LifeLight topic.

Small-Group Leaders Material

The Prophet Zechariah, Sistine Chapel. Erich Lessing/Art Resource, NY

A New Start and a Coming Savior

Selected Passages

Preparing for the Session

Central Focus

The last three books of the Old Testament reflect upon the final phase of God's holy nation prior to the arrival of Jesus Christ. Before we delve into the books themselves, we will review what was going on in Israel during and after the Babylonian exile. Then we will have a better context within which to hear the prophets' inspired messages for our day as well.

Objectives

That participants, led by the Holy Spirit working through God's Word, will

1. identify where the exile fits into the history of the Old Testament;
2. recall the special role that the Lord gave to the prophets who spoke in His name; and
3. take note where the prophetic Scriptures reveal Christ's person and work.

For the Small-Group Leader

Small-Group Discussion Helps

Day 1 • Selected Passages

1. The Lord revealed to the Israelites already in the time of Moses that exile from the Promised Land would be the last in a long line of warnings and punishments that He would issue against them if they should refuse to listen to His Word or "walk contrary" to God in their daily lives. Everyone passing by would know that this once-chosen people had abandoned their covenant and served other gods instead. Before He would send them away into a foreign land, He would first allow enemies to destroy the land and inflict harm, but the sacrifices and prayers of an unrepentant people He would not honor or hear. Yet, once they repented, even in the land of exile, the Lord would remember them and honor His covenant of salvation toward them. After the time of exile, they would return to the land.

2. a. Jeremiah predicted the seventy-year Babylonian exile in the year that Nebuchadnezzar began his rule. The later author of Chronicles credited Jeremiah with the prophecy after he reported that it had come true.

b. God would remember; that is, He would come through on His promises made to His people. Those faithful to Him were comforted that He had not utterly abandoned them. They could hope for a new start as they prepared for the promised Messiah.

3. a. Jeremiah tells us that God called Nebuchadnezzar "My servant" (25:9); Daniel reports that the Lord humbled this Babylonian king in an unusual episode, during which he lost his mind and lived like a beast. Nebuchadnezzar confessed that there is no god more powerful than the Lord and that the Lord alone—and not the king—was responsible for Babylon's greatness. Nebuchadnezzar would therefore not have to see the conquest of Babylon during his reign.

b. There are definite similarities between Nebuchadnezzar and Cyrus. Cyrus, king of Persia, actually names the Lord as "the God of heaven" (2 Chronicles 36:23). God called Cyrus "My shepherd" (Isaiah 44:28) and even used the messianic term "anointed" to describe him (Isaiah 45:1). Cyrus made the surprising claim that it was God who charged him to rebuild the temple. Both Nebuchadnezzar and Cyrus realized in different ways that their success depended on the Lord and that He was pleased to use them for His greater purposes.

4. Answers may vary. It would sound quite promising to hear that no matter how bad their current situation may be, once they are restored to their own land, they will still forget all the shame and sin of their former years. God's face will not be hidden from them, and His Spirit will be poured out on them. Some exiles perhaps would find these promises hard to believe, but faith such as Ezekiel describes comes from God, not man.

5. A remnant is a small portion (such as a piece of cloth) that has been torn away from the whole. It is small only in the world's eyes; the Lord's boundless love and promises protect the remnant from utter obliteration. They are faithful believers, saved by grace through faith, whether Old Testament people or the New Testament Church. The remnant shall return from exile and be established and restored as a mighty nation. Paul in-

formed the Roman Christians of the mystery that God knew the remnant from the very beginning, in order to comfort those who had surmised incorrectly that it was only by chance that they were saved. A believer was called as a child of God in Christ from before the foundation of the world (Ephesians 1:4).

Day 2 • Selected Passages

6. Samuel began his service to the Lord as a helper in the tabernacle. He supported the work of the priests, and every year his mother gave him gifts of priestly garments to wear. God called Samuel by name to make him a prophet, and He gave him specific words to say about upcoming events of divine judgment. This was Samuel's God-given authority, even over Eli the priest, who was many years his senior. As he grew older, Samuel acted as a judge over Israel, yet still remained as a prophetic spokesman who also continued to engage in priestly rituals. Samuel thought it was Saul's kingly leadership that the people rejected, but God informed him that the Israelites were rejecting the Lord instead. Samuel reprimanded Saul for offering the sacrifice because even though he was king, Saul was still required to use a priestly go-between with the people. Thus, he spoke for God as well as to Him, all for the sake of the people for whom the Lord gave Samuel responsibility.

7. a. The people of God themselves were to judge whether a prophet was legitimate or not. The prophet was forbidden to speak in the name of other gods, and if what he said did not come true, then the Israelites would know that that prophet was not sent by the Lord.

b. The prophecy in Deuteronomy 18 was fulfilled in the coming of Christ. He is the One who was to be "a prophet like you," meaning Moses, because Jesus would be raised up as the Prophet (more than any other prophet) from among the chosen people, being born of the Virgin Mary. All that Moses and the whole host of Old Testament prophets foretold would ultimately come true in Christ.

8. a. Ezekiel may have been recognized as a leader among his fellow exiles, but, concerning the call he received from the Lord to be a watchman for the house of Israel, he was asked only to give whatever warning that he received from God. The sinner who rejected the Lord was held responsible for his or her own apostasy, but Ezekiel would be spared only if he was faithful in his task of warning people first. If the prophet neglected his God-given duty, then both he and his hearers would be held accountable and perish in judgment.

b. As it was for prophets in the Old Testament, so it is for pastors to this day. The preacher is not ordered to produce a certain result for the church; he is required only to be faithful in his duties and trust in the Holy Spirit to produce the fruits of his labors. Pastors deserve blame only if they fail to proclaim the pure and complete Gospel of God for the salvation of sinners or refuse to administer the Sacraments in accord with Christ's institution. That is the requirement of their divine call. If a pastor is to be commended, it is not per se because his preaching "succeeded" in growing the Church. It is rather a worthy enough honor to recognize that he served the Lord faithfully. See Luke 17:10.

9. No, Christians today should not expect to receive visions or other direct revelations from the Lord. In Hebrews 1, we read that, while God spoke to the Old Testament people through the prophets, He has now spoken to us through Christ. This means that in God's Word, we truly have all we need and there is no need for us to look elsewhere for messages from God.

Day 3 • Selected Passages

10. When the children of Israel were traveling in the wilderness, the tabernacle was in the very center of their camp. The different tribes were arranged on each of the four sides, all facing the place of God's presence. The Levites and priests lived in close proximity to the tabernacle so they could perform their assigned duties. It was the same arrangement as when they picked up camp and moved somewhere else: the tabernacle remained in the middle of the group as it traversed the wilderness. This arrangement depicted the reality that God was in their midst and they were gathered around the throne of His grace.

11. a. King David desired that the Lord's dwelling place be treated with the same respect and grandeur as his own house—he wanted to build for God a house of cedar to replace the tent that had been in use for about four centuries. The prophet Nathan even thought at first that it would be a good idea.

b. When God said that David's offspring would build a temple after his death, He also promised to establish the royal line forever, including a Savior from David's own family tree who would build the spiritual house of the Christian Church.

12. The Lord had promised that His name would dwell among believers. Along with that promise, He would hear prayer and forgive sin.

13. a. Nehemiah arrived to build the wall of Jerusalem after the temple had been rebuilt. He trusted that, even though the rebuilt temple was simple and less ornate than the original, the Lord still placed His name to dwell there and called it the Lord's house. Even though the people of God disobeyed Him and were scattered among all peoples, He would still gather them and bring them back to the place where He placed His name.

b. Nehemiah stipulated that the people should give tithes so that the temple would not be neglected.

14. Jesus' body is a temple—actually, the perfect temple—because He is the true dwelling of God with people. He is the Word who became flesh and began living among us, walking around with disciples rather than being carried around by Levites, and bearing the testimony to God's covenant not in a golden ark but in His very body. Jesus was concerned about driving out the sellers and money-changers from the temple building because they were becoming obstacles to faith in Him. That was the reason why "zeal for Your house has consumed Me" (Psalm 69:9). He identified Himself with the Lord's house, even as He did when He was twelve years old (Luke 2:49).

Day 4 • Selected Passages

15. In Christ, we have the promise of the new heavens and new earth as our possession now, even though we have not yet attained or experienced the full glory that Isaiah describes. The blessings of eternal life have already been secured at the cross and empty tomb. All the signs of sin's curse are gone because of Jesus' victory, so we have every reason to be glad and rejoice, but for now there is a small time of tribulation and struggle as the present earth comes ever closer to its end. Right now, we trust that the Lord will answer our prayers; later, we will see for ourselves the promised paradise.

16. Daniel's inspired depiction of the End Times includes a period of intense trouble, from which believers would be delivered. Then there is the resurrection and final judgment, after which the righteous will shine like the sun. The book, which belongs to Christ, the Lamb of God, includes all the names of those who will enjoy the Lord's everlasting grace. Moses offered to have his name blotted out in order for the rest of the nation to be saved from punishment, but God said that a name is blotted out of the book only when a person rejects His mercy.

17. a. Faith in Jesus saves us unto eternal life, and that faith is evident in works of love that are shown toward Him as He is found in other people, especially those considered to be in the least esteem. The unrighteous, who reject God's mercy in Christ, similarly refuse to show love to those whom the Lord calls His brothers.

b. Neither the sheep nor the goats in the parable are aware of their good works or lack thereof. In the case of the righteous, their works of love were done as instruments of God, and He left no room in their hearts for boasting or even self-recognition. For the unrighteous, they could not recognize that they were scorning Christ, because they were serving their own selfish ends rather than letting God's love and forgiveness have His way with them.

18. Answers may vary. Most comments in connection with the death of a loved one say that he or she is "in a better place" or free of suffering and pain. Encourage more elaboration on that thought, because there is more involved than just the removal of the fallen world's curse—there is the blessing of resurrection of the body and life everlasting. When difficult trials or illnesses plague Christians, the Lord's presence and promise of full redemption at the end brings peace in knowing that the Jesus who suffered in our world and in our flesh will soon return with a glory so great that we will forget the crosses that we have to endure for now.

Day 5 • Selected Passages

19. a. Samuel was born during the very last years of the era of the judges. The observation that the Word of the Lord was rare meant that, for a time, God did not speak through revelation to prophets. People read God's written Word and participated in the sacrificial worship, but new messages and visions to certain individuals did not occur often. At this time, there was also some apostasy, as exemplified in the evil that Eli's sons were doing on his watch.

b. Likewise, the Word of God was silent between the death of Malachi and the birth of John the Baptist. Many still believed, but many others turned away from the Lord. Yet, as Samuel represented a spiritual reawakening, so also when Christ came, many were called to faith in Him and made members of the Church.

20. a. The fortunes of the nation of Israel turned quite sour when a new king arose in Egypt who did not know Joseph. This might have been an invading conqueror who set himself up as Pharaoh. Knowledge of Joseph

carried with it respect and honor toward the Hebrew people. The new king served only his own power-hungry agenda.

b. Similar to what happened in Egypt, the general situation worsened for the people of Judah as new rulers rose up over them. In the time between the Old and New Testaments, several kingdoms and empires changed hands—from Babylonia to Media and Persia, to Greece under Alexander the Great, to a fractured empire under Alexander's generals, to the Roman Republic and Empire. Of all of them, Persia appeared to have been most friendly to Judea. The Lord used this favorable disposition to arrange for the rebuilding of the temple.

c. **Challenge question.** Answers may vary. It can be assumed that the people would have been looking for the redeemer to come—and also, therefore, for the final judgment and the new creation to come. Life under Greek and Roman rule would have been seen as a temporary cross that had to be borne, but that God would soon bring that oppression of His people to an end suddenly, and with a vengeance.

New Temple, New Challenges
Haggai 1

Preparing for the Session

Central Focus

The prophet Haggai centers in on the largest, most obvious visible indicator of Israel's post-exile spiritual slump: the temple lying in disrepair. Until the Lord's chosen dwelling place is back in operation, He will not act according to His desire or promise for His people. God's blessings and man's sinful, unbelieving rejection of those blessings quite simply cannot coexist.

Objectives

That participants, led by the Holy Spirit working through God's Word, will

1. identify the chief spiritual problem that Haggai was called to address;
2. relate the prophet's words to our own distractions from God's highest blessings; and
3. draw encouragement from the Lord's grace shown to His ransomed people.

For the Small-Group Leader

Small-Group Discussion Helps

Day 1 • Haggai 1:1–2

1. The returned exiles simply said that "the time has not yet come to rebuild the house of the Lord," but there were certain factors that led them to put forward that excuse. There was a lack of pilgrims joining them on the trip back to the Holy Land; in particular, the Levites, who were dedicated temple servants and necessary to the function of Israelite worship, were severely underrepresented (see also Ezra 2:40–42). Certain adversaries, including Samaritans who had settled near Jerusalem, wanted to infiltrate their worship and sabotage the building project under the pretext of assistance. Other enemies sent letters to the Persian kings in order to intimidate the Judeans and force them to stop the project.

2. God's promise came true for the exiles in Persia when King Cyrus announced that he would support their return trip to Jerusalem, specifically to rebuild the house of the Lord. The silver and gold vessels that were carried off by the Babylonians would be restored to the children of Israel, and all sufficient resources needed to complete the project would be supplied. This fulfilled the prophecy that Isaiah pronounced two centuries before, a prophecy that even specified Cyrus by name. God Himself predicted the exile and return several centuries before that, as Moses recorded his parting words to the Israelites in the Book of Deuteronomy.

3. Ezra 1:8–11 lists the returning governor as Sheshbazzar. Zerubbabel may have been the successor to Sheshbazzar; or the name Zerubbabel may have been an alternate name of Sheshbazzar. Either way, he was descended from the line of King David and included in the genealogy of Jesus (Matthew 1:13–16). Joshua the high priest was descended from Moses' brother Aaron. Since these men occupied the two key areas of responsibility over God's holy people, it was appropriate that they were the intended hearers of the divine reproof over the delay in rebuilding the temple.

4. Answers may vary. Procrastination, especially in key areas of one's given calling in life, church, community, and family, may indicate fear or lethargy, among other things, all of which are potentially harmful to a vibrant life of faith. Encourage discussion by asking the group of what specifically someone could be afraid or apathetic of that would contribute to a delay in fulfilling what he or she has been called upon to do. As for the life and work of a church, often a lack of money and willing volunteers tend to be the most commonly identified causes of procrastination.

5. **Challenge question.** Answers may vary. Building projects, especially for congregations and church affiliates, never come about overnight. They take great planning, effort, resources, and long-term encouragement. Discouragement and delays are constantly attacking progress. It can be tempting to misapply the words of Haggai in this chapter and equate one's own church building with the Jerusalem temple. It should not be considered God's will merely to build, thinking of it as though all of salvation history depended on it, for then

one's attention has been diverted away from the Word of the Gospel, which should be the only thing considered essential to the church's existence. Yet, it can be also said that where a congregation is faithful to God's Word and is eager to proclaim the Gospel to its own and to its neighbors, the building of a sanctuary can legitimately be considered God pleasing, in that it would better serve that mission and not become an end in itself.

Day 2 • Haggai 1:3–6

6. The people were revealing that their priorities were self-centered when the Lord pointed out that their own homes were finished—even decorated with wood paneling—while the temple still lay in ruins. He wasn't criticizing an indulgence in luxury; rather, He was pointing out a lack of faith and trust in Him, the giver of all things.

7. Now that David had rest from battle, and the ark of the covenant was restored to Israelite stewardship, his desire was to build a suitable house of worship for the Lord who provided those victories and gave the responsibility of leadership over His people. Nathan gave David the blessing to proceed, even without first consulting with God. Since the prophet was not known from any other Scripture evidence to be derelict in duty, his advice ought not be considered out of order, especially since he pointed out, "The LORD is with you," indicating that since David proposed his plan with a clear conscience toward God, he ought to be free to execute it, barring any future word that might forbid it.

8. King David had it in mind to build a house for the Lord, meaning a permanent temple in the city of Jerusalem. Nathan passed along the message to David that the Lord would build a house for David, which is to say that his kingly line would be established through David's descendants, and the everlasting kingdom of the Christian Church would arise from the ultimate Son of David, Jesus.

9. An attitude of thankfulness is paired with the confession that God has provided all that we need and has given us all our blessings, as David eloquently emphasizes in his prayer. Any gifts and sacrifices that are offered to the Lord need to demonstrate this attitude, or else the temptation to works-righteousness or self-exaltation would have free rein. Selfish mankind may object to gifts of love to God that could be put to more practical use, but the Lord sees the faith that is in the heart producing such love.

10. Answers may vary. Creative discussion should be encouraged along the lines of topics such as publicity versus anonymity, how this gift might affect how others might give in the future, what priorities should be invoked for a monetary gift, if gifts should be specifically designated, what tangible items should be accepted or refused and why. More topics could be raised from the group, keeping in mind the need for an honest, respectful interchange of ideas concerning subject matter that might be sensitive to some people.

Day 3 • Haggai 1:7–11

11. The Lord said to go up to the hills nearby to harvest the wood to use for the temple rebuild. This not only gave them a specific command to follow, but it also assured them that they did not need to search far and wide for materials that were any better than those that were easily accessible.

12. Over four hundred years previously, Solomon had the means to build the first temple with timber from Lebanon, as well as to make a peace treaty with the coastal city-state of Tyre that facilitated the transaction. He also overlaid the walls, carvings, and vessels with gold, which is an option that was probably not available to the returning exiles who were resettling the Holy Land only at the pleasure of the Persian emperor. Solomon's project took seven years to finish; however, the rebuild would need to be done as soon as possible to allow the Israelites to resume their regular sacrifices. The size and magnificence of the building was only secondary compared with the will of the Lord to have a place to hand out His forgiveness and other blessings.

13. By being more diligent in building their own houses and leaving the temple demolished in their midst, God's people were displaying their disdain for God and His Word, showing little regard for any of the blessings that He had promised to them. They needed to be moved to repentance, or they would risk losing their faith altogether and forfeit their sacred role in preparing for the coming of the Messiah, Jesus.

14. A person is rich toward God not necessarily by giving money to the church but by following the First Commandment: to fear, love, and trust in God above all things. If worldly things distract someone from total reliance on Him, then that person is a fool lacking true faith. In the banquet parable, Jesus pointed out that all the various blessings that come from the hand of God can be idolized to the extent that one could risk rejecting Him altogether.

15. *For personal reflection. Sharing optional.* Encourage the group to share their examples. Help the students examine how specifically their time of trial drove them to find strength in God's Word and the comfort that fellow Christians gave when they needed it. Prayer, rooted as it is in the promises that are made known to us in the Gospel, is appropriately extolled as a powerful tool for the believer in difficult times.

Day 4 • Haggai 1:12–13

16. Haggai was the designated prophet who was called to speak God's Word to the people of Israel living once again in the land of their fathers. Not everything Haggai ever said in his life is to be regarded as the inspired Word of God, but only the specific material that was handed to Him by the Holy Spirit for the purposes He had laid out beforehand. This divine call of the prophet assures us that the man's words concerning his assigned subject are the same as God's words.

17. God's presence with His people is comforting Gospel to them, because due to their sins against Him, He had every right to withdraw the shining face of His presence and blessing. Instead, He strengthened them with forgiveness and promised them His help as they continue with renewed lives of faith.

18. Our crucified and risen Savior, Jesus Christ, prior to His ascension into heaven, gave authority to His disciples and to all of the Church to preach the Gospel to all nations. He commanded the Church to train and call ministers of the Word so that those who hear them would believe in Christ and be saved. In this way, Jesus Himself is with His Church speaking His Word, just as He promised, to the end of the age.

19. "How beautiful are the feet" is used in Romans 10 to highlight the fact that the preachers of the Word are intentionally called and sent. They do not initiate the message—their feet are not beautiful on their own. The beautiful words that they speak are God's, so any love and praise directed toward the minister really belongs to the Lord. Yet, God is still pleased to grant honor to His unworthy, but also faithful, servants.

20. a. Answers may vary. If the pastor pauses to ponder the magnitude of the divine authority to care for the souls of his assigned flock, the great responsibility itself brings with it a significant sense of humility. The arrogance that potentially could arise in a preacher of the Word comes not from his God-given authority but from the sinful human heart that tries to abuse that authority in some way for personal gain. While the pastor's exemplary Christian life is a requirement to be qualified to preach and shepherd a congregation (see Titus 1:5–9), his authority does not derive from his sanctification. The pastor is a forgiven sinner too!

b. The class may offer some good suggestions on how to encourage their pastor without necessarily appealing to the sinful nature's vanity.

Day 5 • Haggai 1:14–15

21. In Exodus, God had given Moses the directions for building the tabernacle in the wilderness. Then, as the construction was about to begin, the Lord stirred the people's hearts to contribute materials and skills toward the building project. This work of the Holy Spirit encouraged the Israelites of old to give according to ways in which the Lord had blessed them, just as the former exiles had their specific blessings and talents to employ in rebuilding the temple.

22. Cyrus and Darius were kings of Persia who both employed a policy of religious tolerance toward all the nations they had conquered. Even though Babylon had destroyed the temple and stolen its goods, Cyrus insisted that some people return to rebuild it, and he actually returned the sacred vessels to Jerusalem. Darius, a later successor to Cyrus, searched through the official records to find Cyrus's decree and then enforced it, even above the objections of Israel's enemies in a neighboring province. Working through these two rulers, God employed the greatest possible earthly political force available at that time in history in order to facilitate the Israelite project.

23. Haggai was employed as a divine tool to spur the returned exiles into action and accomplish the important task of rebuilding the temple. In Advent, the Church Year calendar prescribes for the Church to read of the ministry of John the Baptist, because he spurs believers of every age into repentance. As the rebuilt temple anticipated the first coming of Christ, so our hearts today need to be stirred up to faith and love as we look forward to the moment when our Lord comes at the end of time.

24. Before we can ever believe in our Lord or do anything that is pleasing to Him, we need the Holy Spirit to call us to faith and plant within us a love for God's Word. If we were instructed only in laws and requirements, we would remain spiritually cold toward the Lord. Forgiveness and renewal of the heart are the di-

vine work in believers' hearts that stirs us toward accomplishing God's will.

25. a. First, the Christian Church in Jerusalem received the Pentecost gift of the Holy Spirit, as Jesus had promised to His disciples. Second, they received forgiveness of sins and the washing of the new birth in Baptism. Finally, these gifts of faith in the heart motivated these people, on their own initiative, to sell what they had and to care for the physical needs of others. They were all united in one faith, so they would also be united in every other gift that they received from God, including their possessions. This was not an independent action on the part of the congregation, but was solely their response to God's love in the Gospel.

b. Though it may seem that a similar effect would arise for a while if this activity were ever imposed as a requirement upon people in a society, without God's love and forgiveness the selfishness of man would end up taking over, creating more takers than givers—a malady that prompted the apostle to include this warning: "If anyone is not willing to work, let him not eat" (2 Thessalonians 3:10).

The Lord Whom You Seek

Haggai 2

Preparing for the Session

Central Focus

Haggai is not a "one-issue" prophet. The temple is finally getting rebuilt, and yet the Lord has more of His Word to place on the lips of His chosen servant. God is preparing for the dawning of the Christian Church, drawn from all the nations, founded on the death and resurrection of Christ, and sealed by the signet ring of His holy work of grace as it has been seen in the ongoing history of His people.

Objectives

That participants, led by the Holy Spirit working through God's Word, will

1. note how lack of faith was blocking the blessings that God desired to give His people;
2. discover the prophecies that Haggai recorded concerning the Church; and
3. draw encouragement for their own respective roles in the church and the world.

For the Small-Group Leader

Small-Group Discussion Helps

Day 1 • Haggai 2:1–5

1. When the temple foundation was relaid, the tremendous sound that came from the crowd of people attending the ceremony was a blend of triumphant shouting and bitter weeping over how much greater the temple building used to be prior to the exile. Even in Haggai's time, some of the Israelites considered the new structure to be as though it were "nothing" in comparison.

2. The second temple was not going to be as large as Solomon's had been, nor would it be as ornately decorated in gold and bronze. The most important building in Jerusalem could have been easily considered an object of pride for the residents of the city and surrounding area. Some returned exiles, especially the ones who remembered the way the temple used to look, may have inferred that God's gracious actions for His people would now be proportionately paltry. Most of the people seemed to be questioning whether the Lord is indeed present with them anymore. Other answers from the group may be appropriate.

3. King Solomon was most likely very proud of the massive and beautiful structure that he completed as a testimony to God's never-ending presence with His people. But this son of David, as we can tell from his dedicatory prayer, had at this moment placed his faith more squarely in the Lord's promise to dwell on earth despite what the building was (anywhere from 8 to 10 on the scale). The people in Haggai's day, on the other hand, had placed their faith more in the building itself (something like a 2 or 3), rather than in God's promise in His Word. They seemed to let their bad experiences from the exile dictate how they felt God's attitude was toward them, rather than put complete trust in what the Lord had assured them through Haggai and other prophets.

4. a. The Holy Spirit is present in the Old Testament as well as in the New. He hovered over the waters as the work of creation was taking place. King David asked the Holy Spirit to dwell with him as he prayed for a clean heart and a right spirit.

b. Ezekiel was inspired to predict for God's people a new role for the Holy Spirit once Christ accomplished the work of salvation for all mankind. All believers, washed in the clean water of Baptism, would receive the Spirit, who would by grace inspire faith in their hearts and lead them in lives exhibiting faith toward God and love of others.

5. Answers may vary. Emphasize with the class that these three imperatives are not additional demands that Haggai is placing upon the people, but true Gospel words of comfort for the difficult task that lies ahead of them. Like us, they need God's Word to strengthen them, because without that source of strength, all that is present in someone's heart is the fear that paralyzes. The command to work is helpful because it assures them that what they are doing is pleasing to the Lord and conforms to His commandments. With the words "fear not," God Himself is taking away fear and granting a steadfast heart that is bold to do the tasks of one's individual calling in life.

Day 2 • Haggai 2:6–9

6. God shows His mighty strength when He promises to shake the heavens, earth, seas, land, and especially, all nations. Haggai reports that once this takes place, then the "treasures of all nations shall come in" to the temple, which will be filled with glory, even better than in the former time.

7. Haggai's prophecy indicates that a shift will happen with the coming of Jesus Christ. Leading up to His advent, the temple would be reserved only for the believing Jews, who are called as a nation to prepare for Him. After He has paid the price for the sin of the world, then the Gentiles will also be brought into the Lord's house of faith and salvation. All who have been rescued from sin and death and who now belong to God's kingdom of the baptized comprise the greater glory that outshines that of even Solomon's temple.

8. a. The creation of this present time is filled with fallen creatures, many of whom do not heed God's warning through the Word of His prophets and ultimately, the Word of Christ. These unbelievers will perish along with the temporary things of the corrupt world.

b. What will remain is a kingdom that cannot be shaken, and though believers may have to go through a rigorous trial at the present time, they will receive the blessed promise that the Lord will rescue them and establish them as an unshakable Church.

c. Even though our salvation is assured through faith in Christ alone, this does not allow our sinful flesh to take advantage of it and take the abundant mercy of God for granted. Precisely because we have been graciously delivered from sin and the devil, we ought to direct our attention to our Lord rather than to ourselves. Acceptable worship is done only by believing in the Gospel of Jesus, and it is full of reverence and awe because His gifts infinitely outweigh the punishment that we deserve.

Day 3 • Haggai 2:10–14

9. The designation "clean" was assigned to animals or items that were approved for eating or for holy use. Certain qualifications had to be met for something to be considered within the bounds of ritual cleanness. Something clean was used as a way for God to express His grace and love toward His people. Something unclean, on the other hand, symbolically indicated a separation from God, so it was to be avoided. Before an unclean person could be allowed back in the community and in God's gracious presence, he or she would have to be purified from the uncleanness.

10. Death was one of the clearest indications of uncleanness because death is utter separation from God. It is the curse and wage of sin itself. A carcass or a dead body was to be avoided, but when it was necessary to handle the dead, then ritual purity needed to be restored. This was a theological concern primarily, not really one of health or moral principles. However, like an infectious disease, the ritual uncleanness connected with death could spread to other items and make them unclean.

11. The people who heard Haggai's preaching were finally working on the temple and getting themselves back into the routine of the required rituals. However, the Lord was concerned about their lack of faith and their deep-down reliance on their own works as though they were meriting God's favor. On the contrary, every work of their hands, even the things they thought were good in God's sight, were unclean because their hearts were not right.

12. In the parable of the Good Samaritan, all attention rightly belongs to the one who helped the victim, because, like Jesus, the Samaritan had mercy on the one who couldn't help himself. In His story, Jesus speaks of the priest and the Levite passing by, even though one would expect that those who care spiritually for people would also care for them physically. Their greater attention to ritual purity, rather than mercy, is a sign that the Law is inadequate to help us in our spiritual need. Jesus comes as one who was despised like a Samaritan, but with the Gospel He helps and heals where the Law is powerless. While Old Testament ceremonies had a role in preparing for Christ's coming, they would be set aside following His death and resurrection.

Day 4 • Haggai 2:15–19

13. The prophet was leading the people to realize that because they were delaying to rebuild the temple, their lack of faith was also shutting themselves off from the prosperity that they were expecting from God. Haggai pointed out to them that, before the project began, their resources were half of what they expected, or even less. No end was in sight because the vines and trees were not producing, all because the temple was not getting finished.

14. Our daily experiences are immediate, and they take our attention automatically. What we see in our sinful selves and our fallen world around us often crowds out

the Word of God that we hear. But that Word of God truly grants us the faith that trusts in our Lord, despite what appearances seem to tell us.

15. The returned exiles who were listening to the preaching of Haggai in Jerusalem were seeking their earthly treasures without first believing that God would provide all that they needed. Instead of moth and rust destroying their goods, it was blight, mildew, and hail. To lay up treasures in heaven is to believe the promises of the Lord and act according to His will—which for these Old Testament people was to finish the temple and restore the sacrifices and festivals that pointed forward to the coming of Jesus.

16. James instructs Christians to face a time of trial and testing with joy. Doing so gives us a great perspective to know that although worldly things will pass away, the promises of God in His Word prevail and, following the time of testing, faithful believers will receive the unfading crown of life.

17. Answers may vary. People commonly quote inaccurately from 1 Corinthians 10:13, trying to comfort someone when they say, "God will not give you more than you can bear." Yet, that can make it seem at times as though He is far above us and simply throwing bad things at us to test our limits. Even though the passage is actually about resisting a temptation to sin, it would be more effective to add what the rest of the verse says, that our Lord is faithful and will grant the ability to endure temptation, as well as suffering. Showing Christ's love and mercy, reading Scripture, singing hymns, and encouraging one another to confess sins of doubt are excellent ways that Christians offer strength to the faith of sufferers who may be stuck on the Law and treating their trials as though they were punishments.

Day 5 • Haggai 2:20–23

18. Haggai was instructed to tell Zerubbabel in the last recorded prophetic message of his book that the Lord will make the governor like a signet ring. Despite all the devastating events that were predicted to befall all the nations, God will come through on His great promise to send the Savior of the world. Jesus will be descended according to the flesh from the line of King David through Zerubbabel (Matthew 1:12–16). He will be the perfect image of God (Colossians 1:15) and will carry divine authority, much as a signet ring carries the full authority of the one whose image is on its seal.

19. Jesus predicted "wars and rumors of wars" in the last times because the world in its present form will be passing away. The kingdom of God, namely the Church, will last forever, according to our Lord's own promise. Our Savior's stated purpose for these catastrophic events is for them to testify to the coming of the end, and He instructs all believers to regard them as birth pains for a greater salvation that will cause us fullness of joy when all this turmoil finally comes to an end.

20. God promises His support and protection, even during the times when it seems to Christians that He has abandoned them. The psalm points out how devastating the scene will look: a thousand may fall, ten thousand at your right hand; then comes the promise: but it will not come near you. Even when the bad things come and for the sake of God's name upon us we suffer to the point that we feel we are being "killed all the day long," even those extreme trials are actually the signs that we have been made "more than conquerors"!

21. Paul paints a vivid picture of our real spiritual battle, which is not against flesh and blood but against the evils of the unseen realm. Our weapons are overwhelmingly defensive as we ward off the attacks of the devil and those on his side. Our only sword for the offensive strike is the Word of God. That is the armor that Zerubbabel had for the spiritual battles of his time of responsibility, and even though he did not fight for expansion of territory or destruction of enemies, he presided over a crucial time for God's people as they were preparing for Jesus' coming.

Visions of Jerusalem

Zechariah 1–4

Preparing for the Session

Central Focus

The prophet Zechariah was allowed to see a series of visions through which he would proclaim the plans of the Lord that would eventually unfold not only for the Jews of his time but for all believers of all times, who will come from all nations. This work of grace would center on Jesus Christ Himself, for He is the Son of God who came to dwell with humans on earth and to remove their iniquity forever on a single day.

Objectives

That participants, led by the Holy Spirit working through God's Word, will

1. become familiar with apocalyptic passages found in Zechariah and elsewhere in Scripture;
2. link the visions to their fulfillment in the New Testament Church; and
3. receive encouragement and motivation to confess God's name to all people.

For the Small-Group Leader

Small-Group Discussion Helps

Day 1 • Zechariah 1:1–6

1. Zechariah introduces his words of the Lord's prophecy by reminding his hearers of the reason why almost all of them grew up in a foreign land. It was because of the evil deeds of their fathers, which revealed their faithless rejection of God. The new generation, having now returned to the land of their fathers, are running the risk of repeating the same sins and suffering the consequences.

2. As the faithful Israelites would regularly "come back" to the temple for sacrifices and festivals, they were at the same time urged to "return" to God in their hearts also. In the spiritual sense, returning includes realizing their sin, confessing it before the Lord, and trusting in His forgiving mercy. In Psalm 90, the plea is for God Himself to repent—not of sin, of course, but to turn back from His threat of punishment and deal with His people on account of His grace instead. This helps us understand Zechariah's phrase, "Return to me, says the Lord of hosts, and I will return to you" (1:3).

3. In these and similar Bible passages, God speaks of Himself as remembering, in the sense of fulfilling a promise that He had made to His own. When it is said that God "remembers," it usually refers to an extended period of waiting on the part of the faithful. Once that time of waiting was finally over, believers observed at last that the Lord came through for them. Whether it was Noah's family and the animals on the ark, the Israelite slaves crying out to Him in Egypt, or God's people singing psalms in the temple, He acted for their sake in His perfect time. Though Jeremiah threatened that the Lord would remember the iniquity that was committed against Him, he comes back with the Gospel assurance that for the repentant, God "will remember their sin no more" (31:34). Zechariah's name would help remind the people of that gracious promise of forgiveness as well as the established truth that God always comes through on His promises.

4. The priesthood during the time of the Old Testament was limited only to the direct descendants of Aaron the Levite, Moses' brother. Record keepers such as the author of Chronicles were careful to ensure that this pedigree was well documented. Where a genealogy could not be produced, as in the cases reported in Ezra 2:59–63, then those candidates had to be considered unclean and unfit to be priests until their unique situations could be adequately addressed.

5. The absolute permanence of God's Word provides the assurance to faithful hearers that the same truth that saved thousands of past generations will be sufficient to bring eternal life also to them today. The preacher, whether his years of service are many or few, owes it to his holy calling to preach the unchanging Word, whether it seems to be in season or out. When all other things of this world fade like flowers and grass, the last thing the Church needs is novelty in doctrine.

Day 2 • Zechariah 1:7–21

6. In his first vision, Zechariah sees four angels on horses who had just returned from patrolling the earth and were reporting to the Angel of the Lord that the earth was at rest. Following a plea for mercy that was made by the Angel of the Lord, Zechariah was commanded to proclaim that God's favor would return to Jerusalem and its newly returned inhabitants in order to comfort them.

7. a. When the Angel of the Lord appears in these and other Old Testament passages, He is sent from God, yet He is also revered and worshiped as God. He stopped Abraham from sacrificing Isaac, saying "You have not withheld your son, your only son, from Me" (Genesis 22:12). He makes the covenant promises that only God can make. The Angel of the Lord tells Moses through the burning bush that He is the God of his fathers. The Angel of the Lord appears to Samson's parents in the form of a man, yet ascends back into heaven through the flame of the sacrifice that they had offered to the Lord. They confess rightly that they had just seen God.

b. As we pray, we follow our Lord's command and believe His promise. Jesus Himself intercedes for us to the Father, assuring us that by faith in Him, our prayers are most certainly heard. Just as He frequently prayed during His ministry on earth, so also does He now that He has ascended into heavenly glory. His sacrifice in the flesh made Him the perfect high priest, so that once He rose from the dead, our own human nature that He took upon Himself would sit at the right hand of the Father, with constant access to His merciful ear.

c. This One who speaks as though He is God, receives worship as though He is God, and intercedes with God on behalf of His people is clearly the Second Person of the Holy Trinity, God the Son before He became man and came among us.

8. **Challenge question.** Although the foreign nations were carrying out God's will when they defeated His people and scattered them from the land, they were still guilty of a sin against the Lord. Besides raising their hands of violence against His chosen ones, sinful though they were, these enemies exceeded the amount of destruction God had allowed them, and when His anger was satisfied, their power was removed from them.

9. **Challenge question.** In Zechariah's vision, the four horsemen were specified as angels and were sent on a mission only to patrol the earth in the four directions and observe that it was at rest. In Revelation 6, the four horsemen are associated with the destruction of the earth that was begun with the opening of the seals of the scroll. In each vision, the horses have distinct colors, which may refer to their different missions in accomplishing what is ultimately God's will. Horses were the fastest means of land transportation available to mankind at the time; they stood for strength and speed, assuring that the Lord would carry out His Word with power.

Day 3 • Zechariah 2

10. The man whom Zechariah saw holding a measuring line was going to determine the fixed limits of the city of Jerusalem. The angel was sent to inform him that in the days of the Lord's coming salvation, Jerusalem would be open country—like villages without walls because of the multitude of people and cattle that would live in it. There would be no need for a protective wall because the Lord Himself would be a wall of fire all around it.

11. a. Nehemiah wept to hear that Jerusalem was still languishing without a protective wall. This would mean that the city was vulnerable to attack and that the people would not be sufficiently at rest for the proper worship of the Lord in the temple. The people of Jerusalem and the surrounding region were suffering derision from their neighboring enemies and being humiliated by the signs of the Lord's punishment. God placed it in Nehemiah's heart to lead the effort to rebuild the city wall in the century immediately following the completion of the temple.

b. It is not a contradiction that Zechariah's vision is of a Jerusalem without walls—it simply reinforces for us that this prophecy is about the Church, the New Jerusalem, and that this city will be protected entirely by God.

12. God's promise to dwell among His people is fulfilled at the coming of Jesus, who is named Immanuel—God with us. He will make His dwelling as the Word made flesh, and real people will see His glory as He suffers, dies, and rises from the dead for the salvation of the world. We do not work our way up to heaven in order finally to see God—by faith we already now see Him who came down from heaven to be with us, and who promises to remain with us until the end of the age. (Matthew 28:20)

13. a. Our Lord's desire is for people from all nations to join themselves to Him in faith, walk in His light, and combine their voices with His faithful people to praise His name.

b. This new era has begun with the completion of Christ's saving mission and will come to a close when He returns in glory.

c. Christians participate by confessing the truth of God and living according to His Word. In this way, we all serve as Christ's light (Matthew 5:14) to the dark world of unbelief that surrounds us.

Day 4 • Zechariah 3

14. a. Satan appears in the mysterious opening chapters of Job as one who roams the earth, apparently looking for believers to devour, and when God holds up the example of Job, Satan retorts that God has no right to claim Job's fidelity because He has made it too easy. A strange idea of "fairness" seems to overtake Satan. He accuses all "our brothers," that is, our fellow Christians, using God's Law to burden the conscience with guilt. His ultimate aim is to nourish that guilt into full-blown despair.

b. God allows Satan to accuse, even though He has cast him down in utter defeat, because Satan's evil will spur the faithful to trust in the Lord and receive His salvation.

15. Joshua the high priest was, in Zechariah's vision, clothed in filthy garments and standing before the Angel of the Lord. Satan accused him in the Lord's presence, but was rebuked. At the angel's word, the filthy clothes were removed and Joshua was clothed in pure vestments and a clean turban. This vision depicts the Christian's sin being removed and the believer instead being clothed in the pure righteousness of Jesus. Though Satan tries to accuse us, he will be rebuked, while we escape condemnation.

16. The Lord rebukes Satan's accusation and describes Joshua as being a brand plucked from the fire. Here we see that Joshua, who was destined to the fires of hell due to his sinfulness, was delivered from that. Just as a person might reach down and remove a branch from a fire before it burns, so God removed Joshua from condemnation. In this beautiful imagery, we see that our salvation is a gift we receive from God—God plucked Joshua from the fire; Joshua did not remove himself.

17. The Branch is Jesus Christ, the Son of David. To David, the Lord had revealed the promise of a Savior to be born in David's city, Bethlehem, and from David's own kingly "house." The phrase "stump of Jesse" (Isaiah 11:1), is a forecast of the defeat of Israel at the hands of her enemies, yet the shoot, or Branch, will spring up from the holy nation's apparent devastation in order to pave the way for the Messiah. Because of who Jesus is and what He has done for us, He is given the title "The Lord is our righteousness" (Jeremiah 23:6).

Day 5 • Zechariah 4

18. a. The lampstand was a fixture that God had commanded to be placed in the inner chamber of the tabernacle close to the veil behind which was the ark of the covenant. Solomon added extra lampstands when the temple expanded this holy space. These lights were constantly burning to provide a dim light while the priests tended to their holy work of worship. They had to be refilled with oil daily so that their light would not go out.

b. In the New Testament, and the Book of Revelation explicitly, the lampstand stood for the Church that faithfully kept watch for the coming of Jesus Christ.

19. The lampstand that Zechariah saw in his vision was one that not only had a large reservoir of oil that was piped to its seven lamps but also had two olive trees that gave a never-ending supply of golden oil that was transported down golden pipes from the trees' branches to the lampstand. This was a lampstand that Zechariah had never seen before, but once he saw it, he immediately knew what it could do.

20. a. Zechariah's vision of two olive trees referred to the two "anointed ones" who serve the two official roles of the Israelite community—priest and temporal ruler or king. The two olive trees may have brought to Zechariah's mind the two men: Joshua (who was high priest) and Zerubbabel (who was governor and descendant of King David).

b. It is Jesus who fulfills both of these roles now. He is our Great High Priest who sacrificed Himself for us and now intercedes with the Father on our behalf. He is also our eternal king who rules over all creation for the good of His Church. Ultimately, the Old Testament offices of priest and king were pointing forward to our Lord Christ.

21. The image of the New Testament lampstand being forever fueled by the olive trees depicts the Church (i.e., the lampstands) receiving from Christ Himself all that we need to sustain us in the faith unto eternal salvation.

The Coming of the Branch
Zechariah 5–8

Preparing for the Session

Central Focus

Zechariah continues to relay messages of God's judgment against the faithless and a renewal of prosperity for His believing people. Strange night visions give way to the Lord's clear and plain assurances of His presence and a new beginning, claiming Jerusalem and the temple as the focal point for long-awaited peace. God's people are reminded that they are a light to all nations, as the Savior's coming approaches.

Objectives

That participants, led by the Holy Spirit working through God's Word, will

1. take note of a significant shift in the Lord's method of revelation to Zechariah;
2. assimilate Zechariah's predictions of good news with the Gospel of Jesus Christ; and
3. gain motivation for the Church's mission today.

For the Small-Group Leader

Small-Group Discussion Helps

Day 1 • Zechariah 5

1. Zechariah's vision of a flying scroll is explained by the angel to be a curse of punishment spreading throughout the land of Israel. Those who are especially singled out in the curse are thieves and perjurers.

2. **Challenge question.** The dimensions of the flying scroll are the same as for the Holy Place in both the tabernacle and the first temple. This suggests that God's judgment and mercy will be measured out the same as they had been to His people. There would be judgment against sin but also grace and forgiveness through the promise of the coming Messiah.

3. The woman in the basket is identified with "Wickedness." The ultimate form of wickedness is idolatry.

4. The land of Shinar was a region in Babylon. It was not only the terminus of the Babylonian exile but was also the ancient site of the city of Babel, where the people attempted to build a tower in an effort to reach heaven, until the Lord stopped them by confusing their language. Once that action was taken, the people could not communicate to finish the tower and so the people scattered throughout the earth. Therefore, Shinar came to be associated with mankind's arrogant defiance of God.

5. In the vision, the woman, symbolizing wickedness (and therefore, idolatry), is sent away to the land of Shinar. Shinar is a reference to the land of Babylon from which the exiles had returned. Having been in captivity in Babylon, the people of Judah would have been familiar with the idolatry that was practiced there. A house for idolatry would be a pagan temple. In this vision, we are given a contrast between what is going on in Jerusalem (the rebuilding of the temple) and what is happening in Babylon (the building and maintaining of pagan temples).

Day 2 • Zechariah 6

6. The chariots of fire appeared out of heaven to take Elijah away from Elisha. They demonstrated the Lord's almighty power as a testimony to Elisha and to recognize the great role that Elijah had as a prophet and man of God. Later, as Elisha prayed concerning the attacking Syrian army of horses and chariots, his servant's eyes were opened to see the greater might of the Lord, who would fight for Israel against its enemies. Those who are with us are more than those who are with them.

7. a. Babylon and Assyria are considered to be "north country" kingdoms because they had an easier approach to Israel and Judah from the north than if they were to attempt to traverse the Arabian Desert and then the Jordan River. The "south country" kingdom is most likely Egypt. The kings of Samaria and Judah led God's people into idolatry.

b. Jeremiah had warned that out of the north would come punishment for God's people who had disobeyed Him and followed other gods. He later specifically identified Judah's attacker as Nebuchadnezzar (Jeremiah 21:7). In Zechariah's vision, we learn that the Lord's Spirit was at rest in the "north country." This means He had exercised His will toward them and the judgment He had promised for them had been delivered.

8. a. The high priest had a linen turban on his head, plus a golden crown with a signet plate that was inscribed with the words "Holy to the LORD" (Exodus 39:30).

b. The crown that Zechariah was told to fashion from the silver and gold that had belonged to the returning exiles was placed on Joshua's head to testify to the coming Messiah's twofold reign as both priest and king.

Day 3 • Zechariah 7

9. a. The people of Bethel sent two men to ask about their long-standing practice of fasting during the fifth month.

b. This commemorated the destruction of Jerusalem and the Babylonian exile.

c. They were seeking the favor of God through their own works, as Zechariah pointed out to them, and their works of piety were for themselves, not acts of faithful worship to the Lord.

d. If they were genuine in their faith, then they would have heard and obeyed God's Word, acting in love and mercy to their neighbor, especially those who were unable to help themselves.

e. The people refused to hear this and hardened their hearts.

10. Answers may vary. Examples could include the practice of making the sign of the cross on oneself, refraining from certain television programs or movies, or wearing a crucifix. Christians can act in love toward their neighbor by placing the best possible construction on different forms of piety. So long as a person doesn't use the custom as a way to approach God on terms other than solely by grace through Christ, freedom may be enjoyed. Of course, freedom may not be used to compromise the doctrine of Scripture or cause other Christians to stumble in their faith.

11. When Israel split off from Judah in the days of Solomon's son Rehoboam, Israel's new king, Jeroboam, erected an altar in Bethel with a golden calf. He commanded Israel to worship there or at an identical shrine in Dan, and he forbad the Israelites to travel to Jerusalem to worship at the temple. He feared that if they continued their regular pilgrimage to the temple, they would defect and return their allegiance to the royal line of David.

12. Our love does not earn God's love toward us. John wrote that the direction runs the other way: "We love because He first loved us" (1 John 4:19). Loving God means that we believe in Him and trust His Word, but it also means we share that love with our brothers and sisters in Christ. That is how His love works, and He has planted that love in our hearts, along with faith. So our acts of mercy are signs that we believe, but if we resist showing mercy, then we are shutting the Lord Himself out of our lives.

Day 4 • Zechariah 8:1–13

13. In Zechariah 8, the phrase "Thus says the LORD of hosts," is used repeatedly to introduce the separate messages of God's blessing to His people. Occasionally, there is another phrase added, such as "declares the LORD of hosts," or "the word of the LORD of hosts came to me." Each of the words is mediated through the prophet and delivered as though God Himself is speaking. God's Word itself inspires faith in His promise to save.

14. In Genesis 2:1, "host" refers to all of God's creation. He made it all, and He controls it all. When the prophet Micaiah spoke of his vision of the Lord in a throne room, all the host of heaven, namely the army of angels and heavenly beings that He created, were standing around Him. Isaiah's vision included the seraphim, who sang the Sanctus to "the LORD of hosts." The psalm and Malachi both extol the Lord of hosts as a great King over all that exists. The essay entitled "The LORD of Hosts" in *The Lutheran Study Bible*, page 1271, offers excellent material for further study.

15. The statement in Exodus 20:5 that God is a "jealous God" refers both to His threat to punish those who break the Commandments and also to His steadfast love that He shows to those who by faith keep them. In Zechariah 8, God claims "great jealousy" and even "great wrath" not *against* evildoers this time but rather *for* Zion and the holy remnant's renaissance under His grace, as described especially in verses 3–8 and 11–15. God's jealousy means nothing but a good future for Zechariah's hearers.

16. When God promises a "sowing of peace," not only is He referring to Judah's plentiful harvest as He had already foretold, but He is also using that image to describe a spiritual wholeness and completeness (the Hebrew word *shalom*, meaning "fullness, wholeness," is often translated "peace"). Both spiritual and temporal blessings are included in the salvation that the Lord has in store for His people.

17. Jesus Christ, the "Prince of Peace" (Isaiah 9:6), was announced by angels at His birth to have brought peace

on earth because His mission was to secure God's goodwill and favor toward all people. At His triumphal entry into Jerusalem, riding on a lowly donkey, our Savior was greeted with shouts of the faithful rejoicing that Jesus brought peace with God in heaven; this peace was about to be achieved by means of His sacrificial death for sin. In Ephesians, Paul was inspired to name Christ Himself as our peace, since He has made us near, even though we were far off. We are no longer divided by the wall of hostility that He broke down in His flesh.

Day 5 • Zechariah 8:14–23

18. God promised through the mouth of Zechariah a future prosperity of Judah and Jerusalem that would attract people from every tongue and every nation. The people's love and justice would demonstrate their faith in the true God, and it would be evident that God's presence was with them. Many peoples and strong nations would seek the Lord's favor and ask to accompany the Jews in order to take part in their access to His unlimited grace.

19. God's true desire for all people is that they would all be saved, as Ezekiel records. This is His true nature, His proper work of the Gospel, and His antecedent will from before the beginning of the world. The Holy Lord must execute His wrath against those who stubbornly reject Him, not because He wants them to be destroyed, but because His Law justly condemns them. This is known as His "alien work" or His consequent will.

20. When Zechariah lists "judgments that are true and make for peace" (8:16), he uses just a few examples from the Ten Commandments to direct his hearers toward the works that are pleasing to God and flow from a heart that by faith has been conformed to His will. Jesus summarized the words of Zechariah and the Ten Commandments in His Sermon on the Mount.

21. a. The tenth month's fast (occurring in January on our calendar) was in remembrance of the first event of Babylon's attack, when Nebuchadnezzar laid siege to Jerusalem. During the fourth month (early June), they fasted because the walls of Jerusalem were breached at that time. The fifth month (July) included a fast commemorating when Nebuzaradan, Nebuchadnezzar's captain of the guard, burned the temple and took most of the people into exile. The seventh month (September or October) likely recalled the death of the governor whom Babylon appointed over Judah.

b. For seventy years, these occasions had been sad times of fasting, but God promised to turn them instead into times of joy and feasting, because His mercy would so greatly turn their fortunes around.

The Shepherd Saves the Sheep

Zechariah 9–11

Preparing for the Session

Central Focus

Zechariah's earlier visions and prophecies have been building up to a grand reveal of the Messiah, the coming Savior. He foretells destruction for God's enemies, the triumphant king riding on a donkey, the Messiah's saving victory for the faithful people, and doom for the people who in unbelief sold Him off, as Judas would do. Although disaster and judgment run rampant in this section, the focus still remains positive for believers.

Objectives

That participants, led by the Holy Spirit working through God's Word, will

1. notice familiar messianic passages and see them in their original context;
2. verify the true Old Testament hope in Jesus' person and work; and
3. reject the illegitimate expectations of a shallow "gospel" of worldly prosperity.

For the Small-Group Leader

Small-Group Discussion Helps

Day 1 • Zechariah 9:1–8

1. God gave a burden, that is, a prophetic oracle or message, for Zechariah to proclaim against neighboring cities and countries about the disaster that will eventually come to them in the era of time leading up to the coming of the Messiah. Even though cities like Tyre could boast of excessive wealth and protection, they would be no match for the will of the Lord. Other enemy cities would see the example that God would make of these people and would tremble in fear for what was about to come their way.

2. When David succeeded to the throne over the entire twelve tribes of Israel, then communications began between him and the king of Tyre, who was named Hiram. There was a peaceful relationship and trade between the two rulers that extended to Solomon's reign. Without Hiram and the Sidonian timber cutters and stone masons, Solomon would not have been able to build the temple in Jerusalem.

3. The Lord delayed His punishment of sinful nations because, as in the case of the Amorites, they had not yet as a group completed their full measure of apostasy. When that happened, then their destruction would come as He has determined. Even though every sin is an equal offense against God and fully deserving of eternal separation from Him, God is nevertheless gracious and patient, not desiring to lose even one of His own precious children, no matter where they happen to live.

4. a. The Jebusites were listed among the peoples of the land that God had promised to Abraham and his children. Since the Jebusites lived in a city that was very well situated on a hill and well-defended, Joshua and the subsequent judges could not dislodge them.

b. It was not until after David's seventh year of his reign that he finally gained the victory over the Jebusites and renamed their city Jerusalem and their fortress Zion. After that, some were left over from the destruction, so their descendants were forced to work for Solomon in his massive building projects.

5. The outcome looked pretty bleak for the cities and nations surrounding God's chosen nation, yet even some Gentiles were included in God's plan of salvation. Zechariah holds out a note of promise for them, calling them a remnant, along with the few faithful people who were living within Israel's borders. These outsiders would eventually become their own clan within the greater family of the Church, all of whom believe with genuine faith in the promised Savior, Jesus Christ.

Day 2 • Zechariah 9:9–13

6. Zechariah calls for rejoicing because he is inspired to predict the coming of the Messiah, the true king of the Jews, who will bring full salvation for His people. Weapons of war will give way to a lasting peace for all

nations. Prisoners will be set free, and what was once taken away from God's people in punishment will be restored double.

7. The procession described in Zechariah 9:9 is fulfilled in Jesus' triumphal entry into Jerusalem on Palm Sunday, just a few days before His crucifixion, death, and resurrection. Verses 10–13 are reflected in Paul's telling of another procession of ultimate majesty that will take place at the end of the world. With the salvation of the world already accomplished, this second procession of Christ will begin the time when we will permanently enjoy the glorious presence of the Lord.

8. The terms "daughter of Zion" and "daughter of Jerusalem" usually refer to the faithless defiance and spiritual wandering of God's people as a whole. His threats of punishment finally come down full force on the people and the land. The prophet then laments the devastation that has befallen the "daughter of Zion." Isaiah offers a glimmer of hope for the once-ransacked daughter of Zion, and he promises salvation in a prophecy (62:11) that sounds very similar to Zechariah's passage (9:9), and is in fact quoted in Matthew (21:5) together with it.

9. When Zechariah predicts the coming of the great King to the daughter of Zion, he is recalling the devastation of their sins and the Lord's punishment, including the Babylonian exile. They were once beaten down because of their faithlessness, but now they have reason to rejoice, because they will be fully restored in Christ. They will be God's treasured possession once again.

10. Jesus Christ shed the blood of the covenant, which was depicted in the Old Testament through the priestly sacrifice of animals. In order to release spiritual prisoners from judgment, the Law of God required blood. Before, in the time of the Old Testament, blood only signified purification and freedom from sin. Now, our Lord's blood truly purifies us with the forgiveness for which it was the price, paid once and for all on the cross, and our freedom is assured because He fulfilled His promise to rescue us.

Day 3 • Zechariah 9:14–17

11. Following the appearance of the Messiah earlier in this chapter, Zechariah here describes Him as active in battle for the sake of God's people. He fights and protects them, giving them utter victory, as though they are devouring a feast and guzzling wine. All of the actions are the Lord's as He saves the flock of His chosen nation and grants them His plentiful goodness and beauty.

12. In the wilderness, God commanded the priests to sound trumpets to signal the start of holy festivals, especially at the beginning of the seventh month, in which the Day of Atonement would take place. This would alert Israel that God was about to perform a mighty deed for their salvation. When their armies were fighting in the Promised Land, trumpets were blown just before God made the decisive move to defeat the enemy—flattening the walls of Jericho in the case of Joshua, and decimating the whole Midianite army through only three hundred men under the leadership of Gideon, carrying torches and, of course, trumpets, in Judges.

13. The last trumpet, as mentioned by Paul, is the signal at which will commence the resurrection of all flesh at the great coming of Christ. All who are still alive at that time will be changed to an incorruptible form. This trumpet will give us an unmistakable message that God is engaged in doing a great work for our sake. There will be no question that we have reached the ultimate goal of our faith, the glory of eternal life with our Lord and Savior.

14. **Challenge question.** Zechariah refers to God's ransomed believers as jewels in His crown because the Lord values His people as a prized possession. Just as Jesus taught in two of the parables in Matthew 13, so He valued our eternal life to the extent that He gave up His entire glory of heaven to be a lowly servant, and then He gave up His human life, all in order to buy us back from eternal damnation. Likewise, now that we know the exceeding great value of our salvation, we too would gladly give up any of our temporal wealth or glory in exchange for the precious gift we have received from Christ, our Savior.

15. There are a few places in the Bible where drunkenness is a simile for unrestrained, sudden acts of strength and full destruction of the Lord's enemies. Despite the strict prohibitions against literally drinking blood, there are even instances where Scripture describes armies as getting drunk by drinking their enemies' blood as though it were wine! God actually likened Himself to a drunk man suddenly waking up and shouting, in order to highlight how immediate and swift His justice had swept away the enemies of His people. When Israel received the full punishment for their sins against the Lord, it was as though they had drunk a full bowl of wine so that they had staggered under His wrath and punishment. But when the time of chastisement comes to an end, the Lord will remove the metaphorical wine from Israel and give it to their enemies instead. We

should keep in mind that these uses of the image of drunkenness do not condone excessive drinking—they simply highlight the symbolic value of its unique effects.

Day 4 • Zechariah 10

16. Despite the fact that man-made gods and idols were given creaturelike features, they couldn't use their eyes, ears, noses, or mouths even if they possessed a desire to answer the prayers of their worshipers. If there is any message that happens to come forth from these gods, it is denounced altogether by Zechariah as nonsense and lies. People tend to turn to false gods of every variety when their hope and faith in the true God is disappointed because of struggles or they are tempted by an easy road to worldly gain. Yet nothing results from such sincere seeking except aimless spiritual wandering.

17. As Zechariah pointed out, it is the Lord who makes the storm clouds, so He is responsible for the rain. In Israel, the best chance for heavy rain is during the winter months (see the Israelite calendar on p. 262 of *The Lutheran Study Bible*). In late fall, an early rain can help crops get a jump on the winter growing season. Also, in Bible times, it was considered to be very beneficial if God sent a spring rain (also called a latter rain). Unless it was too much and led to flooding, the extra water for the most part gave farmers the hope of even greater abundance. Joel cited the gift of early extra rain as vindication, of removing the effects of the people's punishment, the plagues and insects, and making it as though they had never been afflicted. Instead, they would eat in abundance, rendering their thanks to God alone.

18. As Jesus got closer to the cross, He spoke with His disciples about praying directly to the Father, which they had not done before. He welcomed them to ask the Father "in My name" (John 16:24); God will allow them to pray as though Jesus Himself were bringing the request. And since Jesus ascended to the Father's right hand in glory, that is exactly how our prayers come to the Father's attention. This new access in prayer was opened up when Jesus offered His life as a sacrifice for sin. It becomes our own when we are baptized into the name of the Father, Son, and Holy Spirit.

19. Zechariah mentions that the Lord of hosts cares for His flock like a good shepherd; so also Ezekiel declares that He will punish those who once had responsibility for the flock. Both prophets look forward to Christ's coming, in which God Himself will search for and feed His own flock, the Church. Jesus speaks of being the Good Shepherd because He uses His voice of the Word to gather the flock to Himself. He acts for their salvation by laying down His life for them. He then takes His life back up again because of the authority that He had through His divine nature (He had always retained full authority through His divine nature, but now He also received authority in the course of time through His human nature). Until His final return, Christ our Good Shepherd will not cease to seek out and gather His precious sheep from all over the world, and make them into one flock that follows Him.

20. **Challenge question.** Answers may vary. Encourage discussion on this question, because strong arguments are often heard on both sides of the issue. Be careful not to overlook the fact that both earthly extremes, whether plenty or poverty, are nothing compared to the blessing of having faith in Christ. The human nature, even at times in stalwart believers, tends to take faith for granted and focuses too much on earthly conditions. We are not forbidden from looking for worldly benefits from our heavenly Father, since obviously we receive them from no one else. But if we demand the good things and place our faith in them instead, then we do damage to our relationship with our Savior.

Day 5 • Zechariah 11

21. When God revealed His Word to Zechariah in chapter 11, it was not through a vision or a direct quotation. Instead, the Lord wanted Zechariah to act as a shepherd over God's flock, playing the part of the promised Messiah.

22. The Israelites who reject the Messiah will be destined for the sword. Their promised blessings under His righteous reign will pass to the Lord's true servants, that is, those who believe in Jesus for the forgiveness of their sins. The faithless children's name will become a curse leading to death, but His faithful servants will be called by another name.

23. In Exodus, if an ox accidentally gored a man's servant, then the animal's owner would have to pay the slave owner thirty pieces of silver as restitution. The amount of money was taken to be equivalent to a person who was valued little by the community, and so the chief priests and other Jewish leaders were insulting both Jesus and His claim to be the Messiah when they paid Judas thirty pieces of silver for the life of Jesus, as predicted by Jeremiah and Zechariah.

24. a. The breaking of the Favor staff signified that the covenant with God had been annulled. The Israelites were no longer favored by God.

b. The breaking of the Union staff signified that the people would be divided and set against one another.

c. The sheep doomed for slaughter, therefore, were the Israelites who persisted in their unrepentance and faithlessness.

All Nations Shall Worship Him

Zechariah 12–14

Preparing for the Session

Central Focus

Zechariah's final written prophecy stays focused on the Messiah, vividly portraying Good Friday events and proclaiming victory in His suffering and death on the cross. Zechariah ties these important events together with the inauguration of that favorite prophetic event known as the "Day of the Lord," the time at which full vindication for God's people will be revealed. With this promise as his closing word, his mission to encourage the weary remnant is complete.

Objectives

That participants, led by the Holy Spirit working through God's Word, will

1. apply the prophecies of the "Day of the Lord" to the time of the Christian Church;

2. praise God for the strong witness to Jesus Christ in the Old Testament; and

3. yearn for the spread of God's Word and complete salvation to all nations.

For the Small-Group Leader

Small-Group Discussion Helps

Day 1 • Zechariah 12:1–9

1. The Lord will allow enemy nations to attack His people, Jerusalem, the Church, but He will not allow them to prevail. He will protect and strengthen His people, and ultimately will destroy their adversaries.

2. No grounds exist by which anyone may question Him who created heaven and earth. He was there when the earth's foundations were laid; He measured it out like a master carpenter. If He could manage to set the stars in their places and send rain to remote areas, then our Lord can certainly handle the enemies who attack the Church. He who formed the spirit of man within him will also act mightily to save the chosen ones whom He loves.

3. a. God's anger toward those who disobey Him is described like the stomping of grapes to extract their juice. This passage is the inspiration for the line "He is trampling out the vintage where the grapes of wrath are stored" in "The Battle Hymn of the Republic." The resulting wine, then, is God's punishment by means of the sword against all sinful people, including Israelites.

b. When other nations attack and execute the Lord's judgment against Jerusalem (the Church), then He will make those enemies stagger under the influence of His anger against them.

4. God uses several images of battle to depict defeating His enemies: horses stricken with panic, riders stricken with madness, horses stricken with blindness, a blazing pot in the midst of wood, and a flaming torch put into sheaves of grain. The picture is one of total destruction.

5. **Challenge question.** Answers may vary. What is important to stress here is that the battle is God's, and not our own. He has promised to protect His Church against the onslaught of the "gates of hell" and every other evil. Believers must fight with God's Word as their weapon while awaiting the final appearance of the Redeemer in His glory on the Last Day. His promise of victory encourages us to persevere; it certainly does not excuse us to stay aloof and apathetic.

Day 2 • Zechariah 12:10–14

6. God the Father did not die for us on the cross, so the God who was pierced was the Son, Jesus, after He gave up His Spirit. Peter said, "You killed the Author of life" (Acts 3:15), to highlight the fact that even with human flesh and while in utter humiliation as a servant, Christ was still fully God.

7. The mourning of Hadad-rimmon in Megiddo likely refers to the tragic death of King Josiah, who engaged the Egyptian Pharaoh in battle, even though God had warned him not to. He was the last of the good kings of Judah, the one who had been prophesied (see 1 Kings 13:2) to punish the worship of the golden-calf idols in Israel, and the king who cleansed the temple and revived the Passover celebration. After his death, the people mourned for him, and Judah was soon headed for its punishment at the hands of the Babylonians.

8. Jesus noticed that many women especially were mourning for Him as He was headed to Calvary for His crucifixion. He pleaded with them not to mourn for Him but rather to mourn for themselves and their children, since times of great tribulation would soon come upon them, and then they would need to believe in Jesus and His work of salvation for them. He was assuring them that He was going to His victory over sin and death, not to defeat.

9. Answers may vary. Encourage participants to share their examples. Discuss briefly how each detail mentioned of the Passion history relates to the fulfillment of Scripture and the salvation of the world.

Day 3 • Zechariah 13:1–6

10. The cleansing fountain comes just a few verses after the mention of the One who was pierced. When Jesus' side was pierced in fulfillment of Zechariah's prophecy, the Gospel says (John 19:34) that immediately there flowed blood and water from the spear wound. This was the true fountain that purifies the whole Church from sin and uncleanness.

11. The Levites were holy because they were chosen to assist in the duties of the tabernacle, and later the temple. Their thorough cleansing with water reminds us of our Baptism, which purifies us and brings us into the gracious presence of our God. The Levites bear the sins of the rest of the people, and then they transfer those sins to the bulls in the atonement ritual. Royal priests of the New Testament are empowered to proclaim the excellencies of Christ to all people whom they may meet, and they may also, in their particular vocation, announce the forgiveness of sins by the command of Christ. The Levites were presented as an offering to the Lord in their ritual, but through Jesus' death and resurrection, we are constantly presented clean and spotless to the Lord.

12. The command to be "enemies" or to hate our father, mother, wife, and children, brothers and sisters, and even our own life, is meant in a comparative sense. If we value these gifts of God in our life more than our own Lord and Savior, then we have made an idol out of them, no matter how good our family relationship is. Jesus is our first priority, and He has commanded us to love our neighbors, beginning with our family, unless they insist on being placed on a higher pedestal than our God.

13. Answers may vary. Some common tricks used by false prophets of our day include promises of great wealth, popularity, and love. Even some preachers may begin their message by saying that we are saved by God's grace in Christ, yet they may still deceive us in the end if they require that our commitment to the Lord must in some way earn God's grace and favor. Once the Law (in whatever form it takes) takes over as a conditional promise of divine love, then the unconditional Gospel is drowned out. What makes it so easy to be deceived by this false prophecy is that it seems to agree with the way the fallen human nature operates in this world.

Day 4 • Zechariah 13:7–9

14. a. The Lord allows His Shepherd to be struck down so that the sheep will be scattered. This refers to the Messiah being arrested and condemned to death on the cross, at which time His disciples will escape, leaving Him to face the task of the world's atonement alone.

b. Zechariah's prophecy is fulfilled when Jesus and His disciples are met by Judas in the Garden of Gethsemane. Our Lord Himself first predicted it would take place, quoting Zechariah, and then He predicted Peter's denial. When it finally happened, there was a struggle, but Jesus was beaten and arrested, and then all the disciples scattered. Jesus knew they would flee, so He promised to meet them after His resurrection, in Galilee. This was reiterated by the angels on the first Easter morning.

15. Once the sheep are scattered, then they can be divided into thirds. Two thirds will be destroyed, but a final third will remain to be tested and refined through fiery trial. They will learn through a long ordeal to call upon the name of the Lord and that He will answer them, claiming this remnant as His very own people.

16. Our merciful Father desires to teach us that the sufferings of this present world are not worth comparing with the joy that He has set aside for us, the joy that is ours because of the suffering of Jesus Christ, our Lord. We cry out for help to Him, rather than rest secure in our self-serving idolatry. Our bodies will be redeemed, even though we feel and see them falling apart. He is building in us patience to endure suffering so that we may learn to see that God works all things together for the good of those who love Him. God is for us—who can be against us?

17. Our Lord's purposes for the remnant of Israel are very closely tied in with His ultimate purpose of salvation for all nations. Many of His people rejected Him,

and so He allowed them to suffer the consequences for their lack of faith. Where they were cut off, new children of the Lord were allowed to be grafted into the Church. But the Lord retained enough of the original Israelites who believe that His grace and favor are handed out freely, not on account of works, so that He will be shown to be truly merciful to all who call upon Him. Like Elijah, we sometimes feel alone in our faith. But just as the Lord comforted Elijah with the promise of a remnant of believers, so He comforts us with His promise of new believers in His Church.

Day 5 • Zechariah 14

18. Zechariah predicts some violent attacks upon God's people, the Church, before they enjoy God's protecting hand on the great and glorious Day of the Lord. They will be plundered, killed, and raped, and half of them exiled and the other half cut off from His presence. Intense suffering must precede the promised final salvation.

19. The Holy Spirit inspires Zechariah to picture the Lord fulfilling His promise to defeat the enemies of His people and lead them out of harm's way as a giant who stomps on the Mount of Olives, just outside Jerusalem, and flattens out a valley like an escape route that leads the people of the Holy City to safety. The enemies shall face a final doom that includes rotting flesh and eyes, a plague on their horses and other valuable beasts of burden, their fighters turning against neighbors, and Judah pitching in to help fight alongside Jerusalem.

20. a. In each vision of water flowing, the source is the center of God's presence among His people. Ezekiel, in his vision, was shown a new, symbolic temple structure, with a constant stream of water that started from underneath the threshold of the Most Holy Place, ran past the altar on the south side, and headed east for the Dead Sea. In Revelation, the river of the water of life emanates from the throne of God and of the Lamb—again, the very place where the Lord locates Himself to bring blessing for His people.

b. This prophecy is fulfilled in Christ, through whom we receive the blessings of the forgiveness of sins, life, and salvation.

c. When Zechariah includes the unique detail that the stream in his vision goes both east and west, he means to proclaim that the living water of the Gospel will proceed from God's Church (symbolized by Jerusalem itself) to the whole world in a stream of faithful preaching that will never end.

21. The Feast of Booths, a key event in the prophecy of Zechariah, was originally celebrated at the command of Moses as a remembrance of the Lord's constant presence with His people and His preservation of them, even when they were pilgrims heading for their future inheritance. It was observed on the fifteenth day of the busy seventh month, following the Feast of Trumpets (first day) and the all-important Day of Atonement (tenth day). It occurred in the autumn season after the harvests were done and just before the new planting was to start. It called for a pilgrimage so that all the people could gather together in a holy convocation (in later years, this took place in Jerusalem), and then the people would build booths, or temporary shelters, to live in as a reminder that the Israelites once dwelt in booths while they were being led to the Promised Land.

22. No longer would the Festival of Booths be only a reminder of the Israelites' past existence in tents as they traveled from Egypt to the Promised Land. Instead, when taken together with Zechariah's final message, this celebration would lead God's people to look forward to the Church's expansion into all nations and finally to our future heavenly home, toward which we are all travelling as pilgrims through the foreign land of this world. Nehemiah also notes this festival as a watershed event for an awakening piety that was spreading among the people of Jerusalem and the surrounding lands. Finally, they could sense that God's people had shaken off the dull complacence that was pointed out by Ezra, Haggai, and Zechariah.

Malachi, My Messenger

Malachi 1–2

Preparing for the Session

Central Focus

Malachi is the final prophet to write before the arrival of Jesus, even though there is a period of four hundred years between the events. He is particularly interested in purifying the corrupt worship practices of the priests and strengthening the covenant of love that the Lord had established with His chosen people. Soon, all nations will participate in the plan of salvation, so they will need to rededicate themselves to their holy purpose as a light to the Gentiles.

Objectives

That participants, led by the Holy Spirit working through God's Word, will

1. identify the main areas in Israel's life in which Malachi calls God's people to repentance;
2. understand the connections Malachi makes between ceremony and faith; and
3. give thanks to the Lord for His steadfast love and covenant faithfulness.

For the Small-Group Leader

Small-Group Discussion Helps

Day 1 • Malachi 1:1–5

1. During their sojourn in the wilderness, the Israelites requested that the Edomites permit them to pass through their land. By appealing to them as "brothers" they reminded the Edomites of their common ancestry through Abraham and Isaac. Nevertheless, the Edomites refused their request and even deployed a large army to prevent them from crossing their territory. So the people of God turned away from them.

2. God clearly demonstrated His love for the Israelites by calling them out of their bondage in Egypt and preserving them as His own throughout their forty years in the wilderness.

3. God will have mercy on whom He will have mercy; because no sinner deserves this mercy, it is not an unjust partiality. Paul quotes Malachi in order to assert that a person's salvation does not depend on any human will or exertion, but solely on God's grace that has been given him or her in Jesus Christ. Jacob had done nothing to deserve any mercy—he had even employed deceptive measures to obtain what was not given to him! Nevertheless, God gave Jacob, and not Esau, the inheritance of His promise He made to Abraham, a promise culminating in the arrival of Christ. The "hatred" shown toward Esau is not an absolute hatred that leads to eternal condemnation, but it is a relative term that highlights how great the Lord's mercy and promises will be toward Israel.

4. The Edomites were defiantly challenging the Lord's judgment against them when they made plans to rebuild. Instead of attempting to build an impressive city and tower as the citizens of Babel did, the people of Edom insisted that they could easily recover from God's final word of destruction against them. They refused to fear the Lord, and they trivialized His decisive action against them. Even when they try to rebuild, God Himself will step in and tear down their monuments to themselves, similar to when He confused everyone's language at Babel so that the tower project could not be finished.

5. *For personal reflection. Sharing optional.* Answers may vary. Encourage discussion among the class participants. Not all people will have examples that readily come to mind. Therefore, help students develop their answers by asking for specific words they could say or deeds that they could do for friends who need assurance that God has, in fact,not abandoned them. The Bible's discussion of who was "loved" and "hated" in the Old Testament does not mean that God today, in some arbitrary way, chooses people to bless and others to curse. Instead, because of Jesus Christ, now all Christian believers are counted as "loved" in the eyes of God, even though suffering and hardship will sometimes be their cross to bear.

Day 2 • Malachi 1:6–10

6. Malachi rebuked the priests in Jerusalem because they were offering blemished, blind, and sick animals for their sacrifices rather than the best that they had. This was in direct opposition to God's laws and worship ordinances, and they revealed that these evil men despised the name of the Lord.

7. Ezra and some former captives with him returned to Jerusalem along with some of the worship vessels that had been removed from the temple before it was destroyed. The Persian ruler Artaxerxes gave money and resources to rebuild the temple and restart the regular sacrifices. The people themselves also generously gave freewill offerings to start the temple project. Nehemiah the governor witnessed an oath that the people took, whereby they promised to keep the temple going with their taxes, tithes, and shared duties. None of the regular sacrifices and offerings would be neglected in the house of the Lord in Jerusalem.

8. The traditions of men can be misused to make worship from an unfaithful heart seem legitimate. God knows everyone's spiritual condition, so the flattering lips are not going to deceive Him. Empty rituals are bad because they are done without faith—not simply because they are rituals. They turn things upside down, rejecting their Creator and dictating to Him as if the potter were now the clay. Jesus rebuked the Pharisees and the scribes (so-called experts in the law) because they were trying to nullify God's own Word with their man-made regulations. Impressionable believers may be caused to stumble at the scandal of the treachery of their faith leaders, and all who watch to do evil will be cut off from the Lord's grace.

9. **Challenge question.** If traditions and ceremonies teach and extol the free mercy of God in Christ, then they are most helpful to the Church, and the Lord Himself will bless their use. At no time does anyone who follows extra-biblical directions make themselves more acceptable to God, but those who draw all attention to forgiveness of sins as a free gift from God actually strengthen the faith of others. Traditions may come and go; they constantly need to be examined in light of the Word. When they are correctly and biblically taught, then ceremonies can be most edifying.

10. King David saw that God mercifully ceased His wrathful scourging of the land when His angel approached the threshing floor of Ornan the Jebusite, the spot that God had chosen to be the site of His temple (see 1 Chronicles 22:1). David asked the owner if he could buy the threshing floor and use it for a sacrifice of thanksgiving. Ornan, the owner, was willing to just give it to David, along with all his animals, wood, and wheat. Even though it may have been a sign of respect and devotion toward the Israelite king by a Gentile, David refused his offer and insisted on paying fully. Had David accepted Ornan's offer, he would not have actually been offering anything to God; it would all have been Ornan's offering. Malachi criticizes the priests who use weak and sick animals for sacrifices, because not only are they breaking God's ceremonial law, but their practice of not wanting to give an offering from among their firstfruits also shows a contempt for God. Trying to give an offering that is leftover, useless, or costs next to nothing would even offend a human ruler; to try to give it to God is an utter insult.

Day 3 • Malachi 1:11–14

11. The Lord has it in mind that His name will be feared among all the nations of the world, both Jews and Gentiles. In contrast with the corrupt sacrifices that the priests were offering, these former outsiders will bring what is approved and acceptable before the Lord.

12. When, by their sins, God's own appointed priests treat His name with utter contempt, they profane before the eyes of the world what the Lord Himself has set aside as holy and worthy of praise. These priests are not just making their fellow Jews stumble, but they are also jeopardizing the spread of the Gospel to all the nations. So God curses those who have the ability to bring an appropriate sacrifice but instead intentionally break His commandments with a snort of complaint about how wearisome it is to keep them.

13. While people can measure only the outward things, like the amount of money put into the treasury box, Jesus can evaluate the heart and discern who is giving their all with a cheerful heart and who is making a pretentious show of their abundance. The Lord commends the woman because, in Christlike fashion, she gave out of her poverty and utter weakness all that she had. Even if the rich donors kept on giving and giving, up to the point of surrendering all that they had, their heart would still not be right, because they would still be relying on their abundance to make them acceptable, when Jesus instead looks for faith.

14. **Challenge question.** Believers are free to make vows and pledges to the Lord, as long as the practice remains a fruit of true faith. Churches sometimes like to use information on what people promise to give in the coming year as a way to plan their financial futures with better accuracy. Offerings ought to be given with the prayer that the Lord may bless the gift, purify the heart from all selfishness, and keep the giver's heart fully focused on Jesus Christ and His great gift for all mankind. When pledging and promising becomes a show of sinful pride and is overly focused on amounts that are given, or on privileges that accompany certain good deeds, then there is the risk that genuine faith will be squelched.

Day 4 • Malachi 2:1–9

15. The priests to whom Malachi directed his rebuke were appointed by the Lord not only to follow His commands and offer sacrifices in accord with the Law but also to uphold the covenant that God made with their ancestor Levi. They were to teach their fellow Israelites to fear the Lord, explain to them the true Word of God in its accurate interpretation, and turn the people from iniquity.

16. It pleased God to have Aaron and the priests who would descend from his sons announce the blessing that places the name of the Lord upon His people. This benediction was instituted in the wilderness of Sinai 1,400 years before Christ, and it continues as a blessing for the Church all over the world to this very day. Notice that the Lord's name is given three times in this blessing and that the priests' words are actually God's words.

17. Even though the Word of God that comes from the mouth of a sinful man is still powerful and living, a preacher's false teaching or sinful life still has the potential to do great damage to the faith and life of the Church. Malachi threatens the priests who have been ignoring the Lord's warnings that the blessings they pronounce in God's name will be cursed. The people have already been instructed to avoid, or even punish, false prophets or teachers (Deuteronomy 18:20–22), because they can cause many to stumble and perhaps even give up the faith and perish eternally.

18. **Challenge question.** Partiality is a show of favor to someone on the basis of something other than God's grace and forgiveness in Christ. It also assumes that favor is being withheld from, or unfavorable treatment given to, others who do not have this incidental quality. James uses the ready example of a rich man entering the church assembly and being treated differently than a poor man dressed in shabby clothing. Partiality makes God's people who have been redeemed by the Gospel into judges who insist instead on the distinctions of the Law. When you love your neighbor as yourself, you are fulfilling God's Law because that is the true fruit of faith in Jesus. God gives His mercy to His faithful people so that they, in turn, may show mercy, instead of partiality, to others.

Day 5 • Malachi 2:10–17

19. Malachi noticed that men in the land of Judah were divorcing their Jewish wives and marrying women who worshiped other gods. These men were being unfaithful to both the wife of their youth and the holy marriage to which God Himself was a witness.

20. They were divorcing themselves not just from their wives but also from what God had intended for them. By then marrying pagan women, the Israelite men were demonstrating an acceptance of idolatry.

21. Moses allowed a man to divorce his wife on the condition of her infidelity to him, or for some form of indecency that would be tantamount for desertion. Jesus cites this as a concession because of the peoples' hardness of heart. He seems to make the requirement more strict by forbidding the husband to marry anyone else after a divorce (except in cases of marital unfaithfulness or sexual immorality). Jesus isn't really changing the Law, but He is pointing out that divorce is not God's plan for the holy estate of marriage.

22. Ephesians states that husbands are to love their wives as Christ loved the Church, so if infidelity happens as described by Malachi, that image of Jesus that is found in marriage becomes grossly marred. If a believing husband practices infidelity, he is actually despising his own body, since before God he was joined as one flesh with his wife. The husband made a lasting covenant with the wife of his youth, reminiscent of the unbroken promise of love from our Savior. If that holy bond is broken in malicious desertion, then that marriage brings dishonor to Christ.

The Coming Messenger

Malachi 3–4

Preparing for the Session

Central Focus

Malachi's final prophetic messages are meant to inspire faith among the people living in the newly rebuilt Judah and Jerusalem. He departs from the topic of priestly corruption to highlight the coming of the promised Messenger and those who would prepare ahead of Him. After he urges repentance upon a faithless and selfish nation, Malachi promises a great and final day of salvation for believers, but destruction for the wicked.

Objectives

That participants, led by the Holy Spirit working through God's Word, will

1. perceive the need for repentance when their lives reflect a lack of faith;
2. look forward joyfully to the continuous coming of the Savior for forgiveness; and
3. be encouraged to continue studying the Bible and discover more of its riches!

For the Small-Group Leader

Small-Group Discussion Helps

Day 1 • Malachi 3:1–5

1. John the Baptist is foretold by the prophet Isaiah (40:3) to be the voice that cries, "In the wilderness prepare the way of the Lord." The Gospels cite this passage to describe how John preached to the people to prepare their hearts for the Christ and His coming kingdom. John's father, Zechariah the priest, had predicted in his song the *Benedictus* that in preparing the way for the Lord, John would also share knowledge of salvation to those who would believe in Christ for the forgiveness of sins. The Gospel of John informs us that John the Baptist understood his own role to decrease as Jesus' role increased, and he allowed his disciples to stop following the "best man" because now the "Bridegroom" had finally arrived.

2. Malachi was inspired to predict the coming of the Lord, that is, the Messiah, to His temple. This is more than just the building in Jerusalem, which Jesus visited many times during His life, of course; this is the temple of His human body that He would now inhabit (John 2:21). He will spiritually cleanse and purify His servants, the sons of Levi, and sit in judgment over them for their deeds.

3. a. The sons of Levi (i.e., the priests and temple servants) will be purified like gold and silver by the Lord, the Messenger of the covenant.

b. The access of this limited group of Old Testament people to the holy presence of God will in the New Testament era be extended to all believers, making all baptized Christians into royal priests, God's chosen people (1 Peter 2:9). By faith, through which the saints accept the promises of the Lord and are granted the forgiveness that Jesus earned, these new "sons of Levi" will not be offering ceremonial offerings in a certain way, but they will offer their very lives as a gift of righteousness, perfect in God's sight. The faith of early Israel was not absolutely perfect, but it was stronger than it was later on in Malachi's day. Yet, the same renewed faith is also promised to all believers, because Jesus' own faith was perfectly pleasing to the Father, and just as for Abraham, that faith is counted to us as righteousness (Romans 4:3).

4. **Challenge question.** Answers may vary. The word "suddenly" comes true in the surprise that the shepherds had at the revelation of the angels, the shock that King Herod and the people of Jerusalem had at the arrival of the Wise Men, and the astonishment of the people at the preaching and miracles of Jesus. Even with John's preaching to prepare them, the appearance of the Lord still comes as a surprise because many judge on appearances rather than trust in what the Word of God says. Just as suddenly, though, our Lord will return at the end of the world, though no one knows the day or the hour. May we also, by God's grace, keep the faith that we have been given so that we may always watch for Him at all times!

Day 2 • Malachi 3:6–11

5. The tithes in the Old Testament were contributions of the best parts to the Lord, but they were also meant for the sustenance of the Levites, as part of their inheritance in serving the Lord. The Levites did not have their own land to produce their own food, so they received the tenth part of what their relatives in other tribes produced. In turn, the Levites gave a tenth of their receipts for the priests to live on, since they too worked among God's people. Nehemiah renewed the tithing practice that had died out in Israel, and he emphasized the rise of music in worship, thanks to the regular contributions of the holy people. The temple servants had time to serve the people, and the people were spared the burden of God's wrath because they were not allowed to approach His presence on their own—rather, they were to be represented by the Levites and priests who received their tithe.

6. The idea of robbing God is that people are withholding their promised and required gifts from Him. Keeping what really belongs to Him is no different than stealing from the Lord.

7. God forbids anyone at any time from putting Him to the test when the object is to deny His existence or lordship. Satan tempted Jesus with various vestiges of glory in the hopes of tearing Him away from the mission of salvation. He was, of course, reproved from Scripture spoken straight from the mouth of Scripture's Author. When God desires to quicken a believer's faith and release a flood of blessing, then He invites that "doubting Thomas" to test, touch, and experience what abundant love He has in store for the believer. This testing isn't challenging God, but "tasting" to see that the Lord is good.

8. a. The old ritual obligations, including the tithe, were fulfilled in Christ Jesus and so have passed away. Therefore, we are under no obligation to give a strict ten percent. We are free to give either less or more than ten percent.

b. By collecting for the relief of the poor and needy, we can demonstrate the love that we have both for God and also for others. Likewise, by contributing for the maintenance of the church building and the support of the clergy, we are showing our reverence for God by ensuring (through earthly means) that His grace may continue to be distributed among us through Word and Sacrament.

9. **Challenge question.** Answers may vary. The difference is in the attitude of faith. If one approaches giving with demands for God's blessings based on one's own works righteousness, then the gift is actually an offense against the Lord. If, on the other hand, one is full of faith and confident of the heavenly Father's abundant blessings of body as well as soul in Christ, then one's offering is not perceived as a payment for those blessings but rather a small thanksgiving for what has already been received.

Day 3 • Malachi 3:12–15

10. If the people of God would obey His voice, then He would send blessings that would overtake them, and He would place them high above all other nations, who would then take notice. All enemies would be defeated, everything that produced food for Israel would be plentiful, and the people themselves would be fruitful and multiply, as would their livestock. Rain would come at the proper times, and the people would be given the Lord's generosity in order to share His goodness with others—they will lend and not borrow. All of this will proclaim to the other nations that the Lord is the one true God and that He will send salvation to the world through the nation of Israel (John 4:22).

11. When we notice that worldly advantages come to those who are opposed to God's will, we may pray as Jeremiah did for their ultimate accountability to judgment. The Lord's prior promises will hold true, and His chosen people (along with any foreigners who convert) will finally obtain their inheritance. The psalmist fully admitted to the Lord his envy over the prosperity of the wicked, but he emphasized how his enemies were offending God most of all. He found perfect understanding when he went into the holy sanctuary for worship—he knew then that the Lord would act justly against His enemies. Even though flesh and heart may fail, God is always going to be the strength of our hearts and also our refuge.

12. The prodigal son returned, and the father ran to embrace him and welcome him home with the best possible feast—the fatted calf. The older brother felt as though he had received nothing, even though he never left home and never squandered his wealth, as he so readily points out! Yet, he resented the generosity of his father toward his brother because he felt in some way that the prodigal didn't deserve any love, especially after what he had done. The older son claimed to have

been a slave to his father without receiving one ounce of recognition or the freedom to celebrate separately with friends in return. He didn't address his father with respect, and the story ends with a decision placed in his lap—will he celebrate God's grace for a sinner (his brother)? Or will he stay away and keep insisting on salvation by works instead?

13. The workers who bore the heat of the day in the vineyard had already agreed to their wages. When they were lined up after work to get paid, they noticed that the ones who were last hired were paid the same amount as they were, and then they were upset because they did not receive more. We also can be distracted by the Law's constant measurements and comparisons so much that we fail to see the true "unfairness" of the Gospel. When we are constantly reminding ourselves that we are most unworthy of God's love, yet we receive it anyway, then we are more likely to remain content when we see instances of His love toward others who are just as unworthy.

Day 4 • Malachi 3:16–18

14. God promised that those who feared Him would be placed in a book of remembrance and would be regarded as His treasured possession. The Lord will spare them when His appointed day of judgment arrives, and they will speak the comfort of God's Word to one another.

15. The apostle Paul greets the congregations in and near the city of Corinth in the name of the Father of mercies and God of all comfort. He speaks words of comfort to us in the name of Jesus Christ, so He has it in mind that we would speak comfort to anyone who is suffering affliction. Our comforting words do not originate with anything we have done, but are rather the same comforting words that we have received from our Lord in His Word.

16. Answers may vary. Any sort of crisis may be an opportunity for a church to be strengthened in the faith, but for that to be done, that congregation would need to receive comfort from Christ in His Word. Adversity by itself does not strengthen us, nor do we look within ourselves to see us through—our suffering must point us away from ourselves and to our Lord alone. If we follow the temptation to doubt God and refuse His comfort, then the time of trial will indeed be insurmountable.

17. **Challenge question.** A book of remembrance was used by a king or other leader to establish a public record that could not be reversed, unless a permanent change necessitated a name to be blotted out of the book. When a name was recorded in this book, therefore, then the action of the ruler for the sake of that person was guaranteed. God, in His omniscience, does not actually need anything written down to remind Him (as we do!), but out of love He accommodated Himself to this image to assure His faithful people that He will fulfill His promises toward them perfectly—without fail!

18. a. The Hebrew numbering of the verses in Malachi suggest that chapter 4 will keep going with what is promised here at the end of chapter 3. The Day of the Lord will be a burning oven that will consume the stubble, the unusable stalks and chaff left over after a harvest, which refers to the wicked unbelievers. The righteous will tread on their ashes, leaping around in joyful release like a young calf breaking loose from a confining stall. Christ "the sun of righteousness" will rise, not to burn the faithful with His heat of judgment, but to provide healing wings to bind up the brokenhearted.

b. Through faith in Christ, we are covered in Jesus' own perfect righteousness and are just and innocent in the eyes of God.

Day 5 • Malachi 4

19. The Lord has ordained perfect peace for those who stay their minds (Isaiah 26:3) on Him. Those who refuse God's gifts but remain anyway in the land of uprightness will not see the majesty of the Lord when the Day of Judgment comes. Other oppressive lords have done their worst, but they will pass away, due to God's own promised destruction of the wicked. He will surely increase the nation of the blessed faithful, and through faith in Christ that is nourished in His Word of forgiveness, the Lord will enlarge the borders of His Church when and where He pleases.

20. Moses recorded the Law that the Lord had instructed His people of all ages to keep and His Word of promise to believe in true faith. Moses himself gave the Law to the people who would enter the Promised Land, even though he was permitted only to see it but not to enter it. Yet, God still for all time considered Moses to be His servant; He did not make him forfeit that distinctive title. So that would tell us that to partake fully of our Lord's promises we should look to One who was greater than Moses—namely, Jesus.

21. John the Baptist fulfilled Malachi's prophecy of Elijah the prophet when he cried out in the wilderness for people to repent. Together with his preaching, he baptized in the Jordan River, the boundary between the Promised Land and the wilderness—highlighting a transfer of the baptized believer from God's condemnation to His blessing. John could immediately see that there were hardened hypocrites who were mixed in with those who wanted Baptism. For them, he urged proper repentance and for them to bear genuine fruit. When other people heard this, they were properly convicted in spirit and overwhelmed, so John guided them in the way of the Ten Commandments as to what works of repentance they should do in their individual callings in life.

22. Like Elijah and Malachi, John the Baptist preached within the Promised Land. He urged God's people to repentance, which would turn fathers to their children and children to their fathers, honoring the particular vocations in which they were to observe the Law of Moses, and all the while preparing their hearts to confess their sins and believe in the Messiah.